A publication for elementary children (6-8 years of age).

STUDENT ACTIVITY WORKSHEETS YEAR 1

Corresponds to Year 1 of the cycle of three years of Elementary lesson books.

I0161687

ELEMENTARY

Elementary 1 - Student Activity Worksheets

Published by:
Mesoamerica Region Discipleship Ministries
www.SDMIresources.mesoamericaregion.org

ISBN: 978-1-63580-070-8

All of the scripture verses quoted are from the NIV Bible.

Translated into English from Spanish by:
Bethany Cyr

Printed in the United States

Mesoamerica Region

TABLE OF CONTENTS

What happened after?

1

2

God's Guide

3

4

Tell your family and friends about how God led Moses.

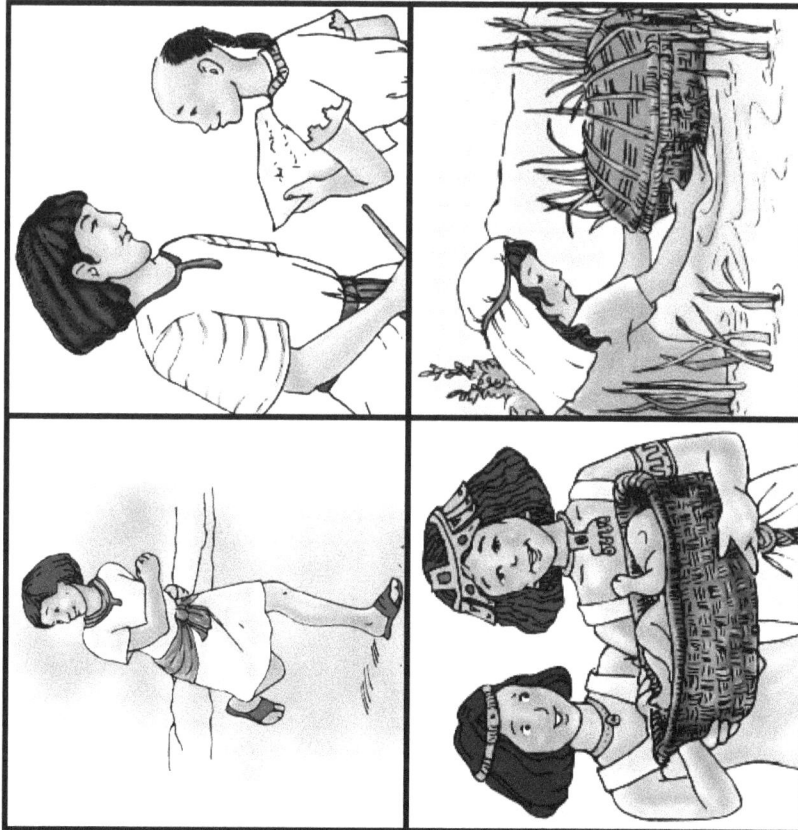

Cut out the four pictures.
Paste them in the boxes in the order
In which the story happened.

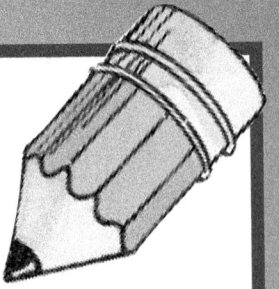

The funny pencil

Follow the instructions to find the words that should go in the lines below:

In line 1, circle the toys.
In line 2, circle the foods.
In line 3, circle the animals.
In line 4, circle the colors.
In line 5, circle the plants.

1. doll   truck   God   ball
2. apple   has   milk   bread
3. cow   dog   cat   plans
4. for   green   blue   red
5. tree   flower   you   grass

Write the words you had left over in the lines below.

_____ _____ _____ .

The burning bush

Color the bush green. Fold down on the dotted lines and use the picture to tell someone today's Bible story.

Color the fire in the bush.

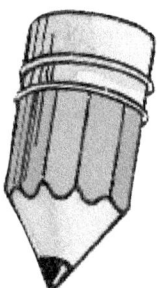

The funny pencil

Find the special message from God for you.

10 9

7   6   5   11   12

2

8   3   1   4

God needs ___ 1   12   11   11   5   2   12   6   5   4   12   6   10

You can ___ 2   9 ___ **one also.**

God helps those who obey ___ 7   3   8 .

Write the name of each picture on the lines after the pictures. Then write the letters that are inside the circles on the lines that have the same number in the sentences below.

8

Action in the Red Sea

Look for instructions on the back of this sheet.

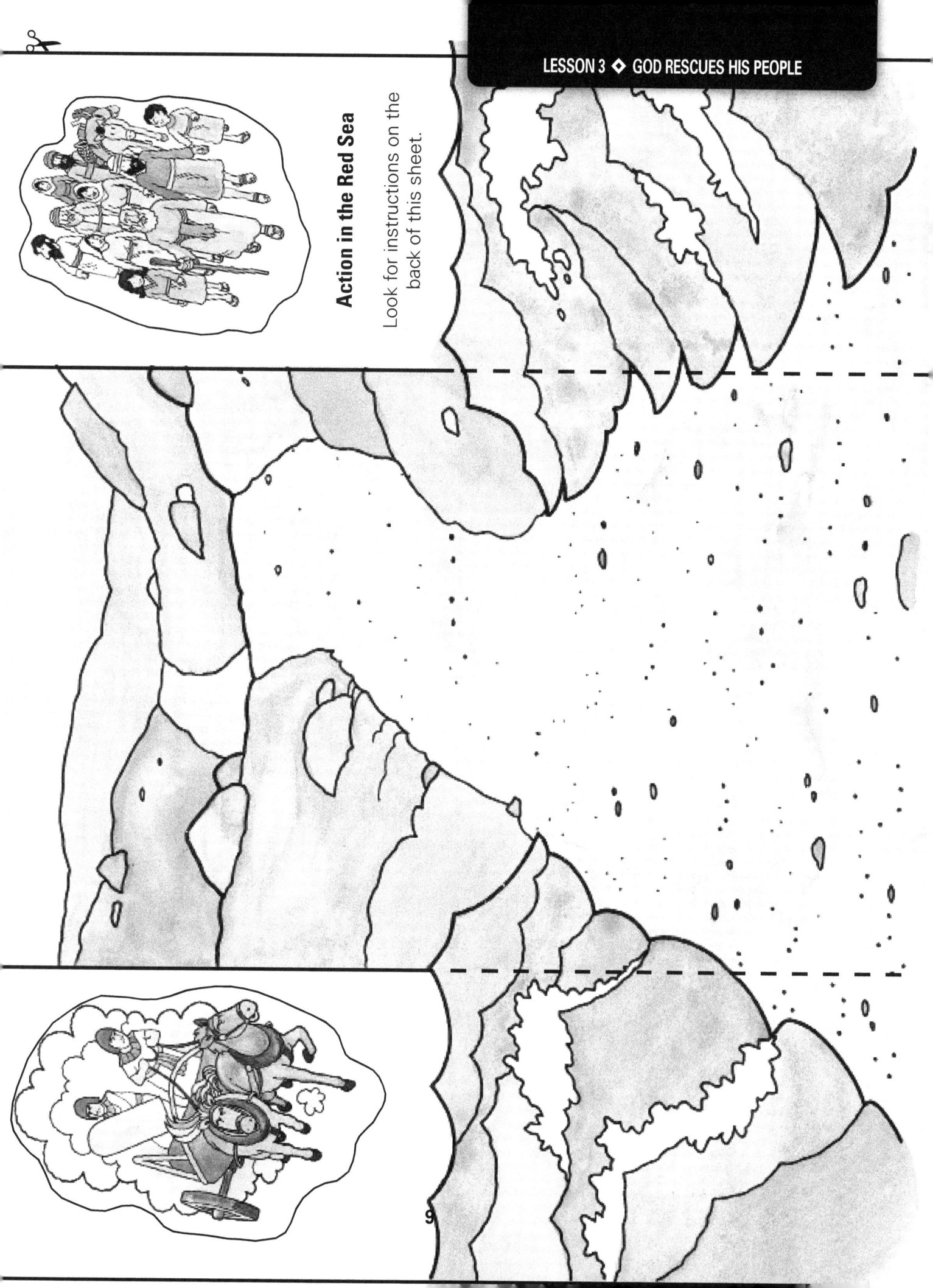

9

Cut along the solid black lines above the water and along the edges. Fold forward on the dotted lines. Cut out the Israelites and the Egyptians. Use them to remember the Bible story. Open the water to let Moses lead the Israelites across the Red Sea. Fold in the water part so that you see how God saved his people from the Egyptians.

"Hit the rock with your staff and water will come out of it for the people to drink" (Exodus 17:6 - paraphrased).

God provides water for his people.

Connect the dots to find out what miracle God performed for His people. Look on page 119 for Moses' arm and put it in the right place using a brass fastener or clasp. Color the picture.

11

God Loves You

Give _____ _____ to the _____ _____, for he is _____, His _____ _____ endures _____ _____ _____.

(Psalms 136:1)

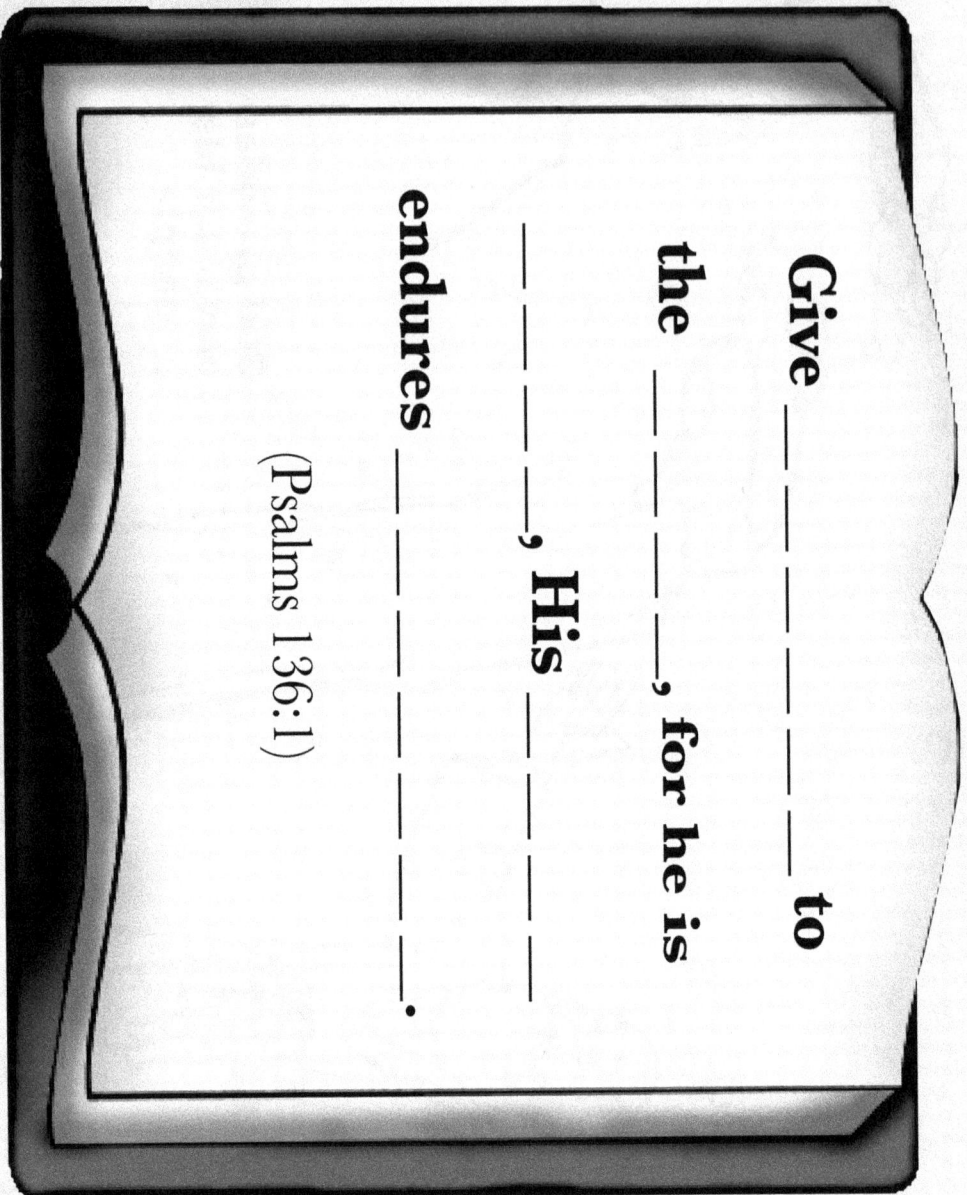

Use the following words to complete the verse:

Thanks
Lord
Good
Love
Forever

Discuss with your students what this verse means. Encourage your students to keep this worksheet as a reminder to thank God for his infinite love.

I want to Love and Obey God

God gives us his laws so we can live the right way. He helps us every day. I will obey him because I love him.

This week I will:

_____

Name

Sunday  Tuesday  Thursday  Saturday

 Monday  Wednesday  Friday

Draw two pictures that show how you can obey God this week. Cut off this instruction strip and poke holes through the black circles at the top of the worksheet. Put a ribbon or string through the holes and secure it with tape, so that you can hang the worksheet up in your house. Color a star each day that you fulfill what you have promised.

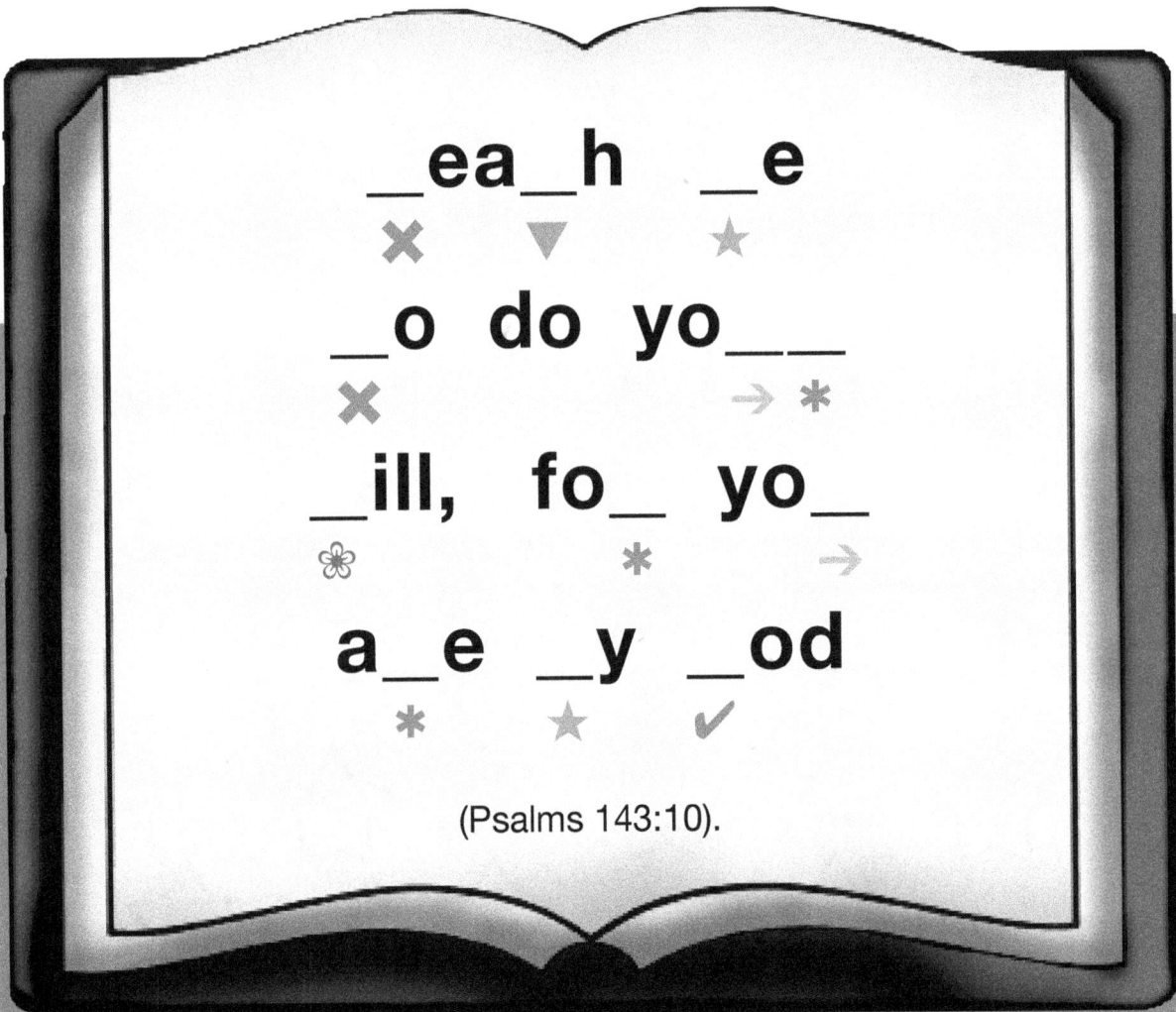

Code for the Bible verse

Complete the Bible verse by using the code.

_ea_h _e
_o do yo___
ill, fo yo_
a_e _y _od

(Psalms 143:10).

Can you repeat this verse?

Write a Story

"You shall have not other gods before me".
(Exodus 20:3)

"You shall not bow down to them or worship them".
(Exodus 20:5a)

"You shall not misuse the name of the Lord your God".
(Exodus 20:7a)

"Remember the Sabbath day by keeping it holy".
(Exodus 20:8)

Create two stories for each picture. In the first story, tell about a person who disobeys God, and in the second, tell about a person who keeps God's commandments.

15

Pictures and Vowels

Complete the Bible verse below by writing in the vowel that is the first letter of the name of the picture (elephant = e).

octopus   ice cream   umbrella   apple   elephant

bey th Lord yo_r

G_d and foll_w

h_s c_mm_nds

_nd decre_s.

D_ut_ron_my 27:10

Please John, put your bicycle where it belongs.

glue here.

We Honor Our Parents

Discuss what the drawings on this activity sheet represent.
Cut out the pictures on page 119 that show the correct way to act and glue them in the appropriate place.
In the empty frame below, draw a picture showing some way that you can honor your parents this week.

glue here.

The Labyrinth of Letters

Follow the lines to find the missing words in the story below.

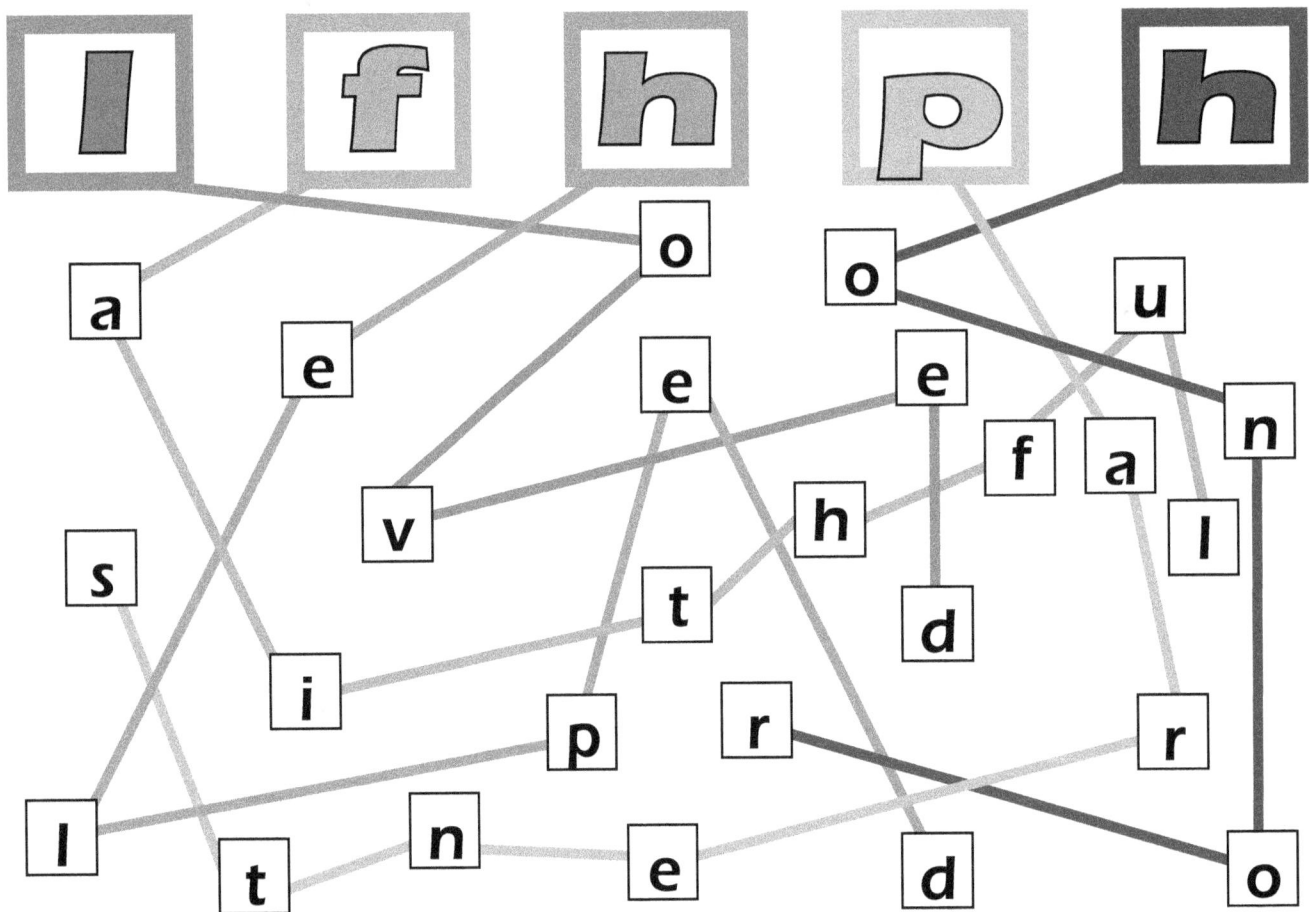

■ David _ _ _ _ _ his parents.

■ He was always _ _ _ _ _ _ _ _ _ to them.

■ David _ _ _ _ _ _ his father take care of the sheep.

■ When David grew up, he looked for a safe place for his _ _ _ _ _ to live.

■ I can be like David when I _ _ _ _ _ my mom and my dad.

18

The different faces of the Robber

Cut out the different faces found on page 117 in your book. Look at the first 3 pictures. Decide how Rachel's face was seen in the different events of the story. In each box, paste the face that you think best expresses Rachel's feelings. Follow the instructions in the last box.

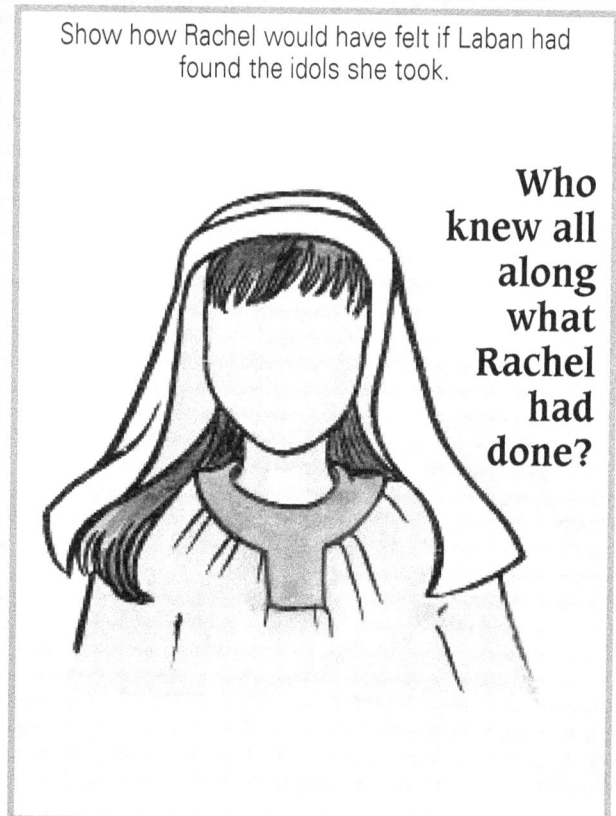

My father deceived us, we deserve to have these idols.

No one noticed the theft.

I hope my father does not see anything in these saddle bags.

Show how Rachel would have felt if Laban had found the idols she took.

Who knew all along what Rachel had done?

19

Would you do that to someone you love?

Draw a ⊘ around the pictures that show something you would not do to a person you love. Think about and tell your friends how the Ten Commandments help us to put love into practice.

Love 🤍 does no ⊘ harm to a neighbor.

Therefore love ❤️ is the fulfillment of the law.

Romans 13:10

Naboth's Vineyard

Number the pictures according to the Bible Story your teacher told you. Then talk with your friends in class about what happened in the story and which of God's commandments was not obeyed.

If we think incorrectly, we will act incorrectly. Where did King Ahab's problem begin?

wanting   did it all   drinking

seeing   Where   coveting   begin?

Be a super star!

Cut out the stars on page 119. Read each story or listen carefully while your teacher reads the stories out loud. Glue a star in the blank space after each story that talks about a person who obeys the commandments of God.

Daniel found Mario's ball in the bushes and decided to keep it because he likes it more than he likes his own ball.

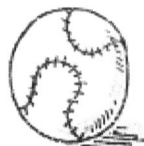

Ana kicked her brother's favorite toy airplane and broke it. But she confessed the truth and apologized and then she helped him repair it.

Marcos found some money on the playground at school that someone had dropped. He gave it to his teaher so that she could return it to the owner.

Rosita lost a piece of her sister's puzzle, but she told her sister that their little brother was the one who had lost it.

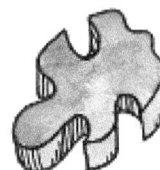

Luis told his father that the dog had trampled the flowers in the garden when it had acutally been Luis who did it. Later, Luis asked Jesus for forgiveness for having lied and he told his father the whole truth.

Pedro wants to go and play at the house of his friend Miguel. He told his mother that he had finished his homework, but the truth is that he only did half of his homework and later plans to do the rest.

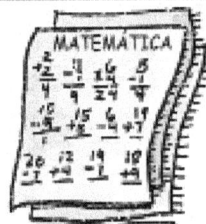

Lily saw that Emma forgot her doll at church. Lily really likes Emma's doll, but she's going to find her friend Emma and return the doll to her.

Jesus gave us an example of love and service.

"I have set you an _____ _____ done for you." (John 13:15).

that you should do as I have

Write the missing word in the blank spaces of the scripture verse. Color the picture. Then turn the page over and cut along the black lines. Then put the puzzle together with your friends and tell them the story you learned today.

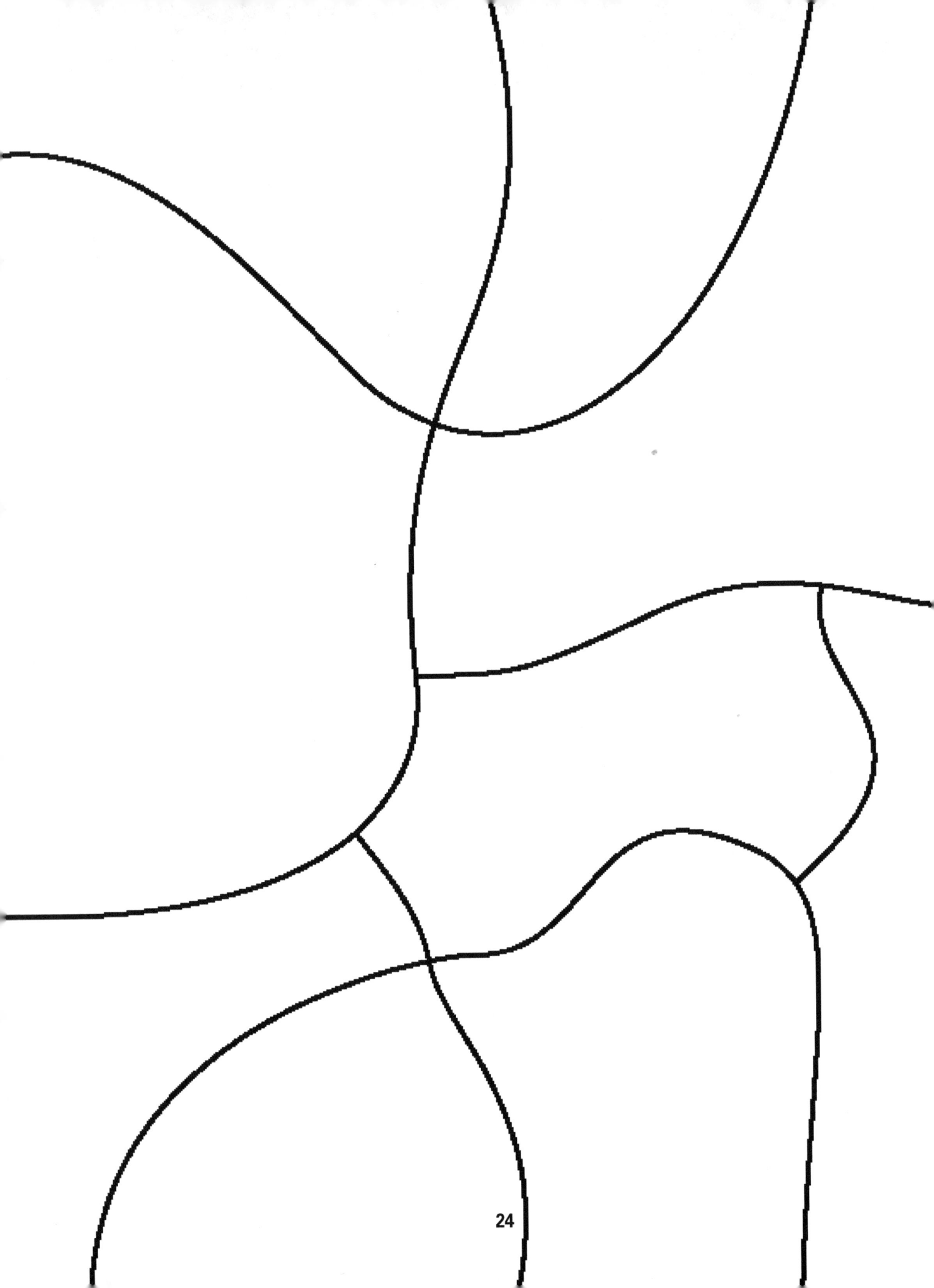

The prayer of Jesus

1. "Abba" Father.

Please take the suffering away from me.

2. Please, hurt them before they hurt me.

5. I did what you wanted, now you do what I want.

3. Your are able to do all things.

6. I will do what you want me to do, not what I want.

Read each of the above phrases. Draw a circle around the phrases Jesus used while he was praying to God, his father.

The Prayer Cube

↑5 Accept what God wants.

How to make the Prayer Cube.

Cut along the solid black lines and fold along the dotted lines. Paste sides A, B, and C under side 1: "We pray to God". Paste sides D, E, and F under side 6: "We pray to God". Fold the G and H tabs inside the cube and glue. The cube will help you remember how you should pray.

D

↑4 Tell Him what you want.

B

E

↑3 Tell God how you feel.

C

F

1 Pray to God.

Tell God how much you love him.

2 Praise God for His power.

6 Pray to God.

Tell God how much you love him.

Why did Jesus Suffer for Us?

What did Jesus do when he was treated unfairly? Draw a line from the phrase to the picture that tells us what Jesus did.

Jesus decided to follow God's plan.

Jesus forgives his enemies.

Jesus tells the truth.

"And Jesus said: 'Father, forgive them, for they know not what they do'..."

(Luke 23:34)

27

"But God demonstrates

his own love

for us in this:

While we were

still sinners,

Christ died

for us."

(Romans 5:8).

Cut out each of the squares with drawings on them and the rectangles containing the scripture verse. Glue them on a piece of cardboard or construction paper to make a poster to help you remember what you learned today.

Forgiven

Jesus

Color and decorate the words
"Jesus" and "forgiven".

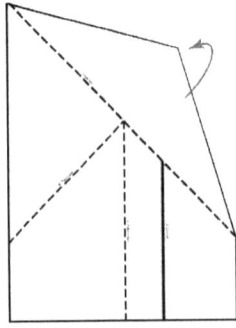 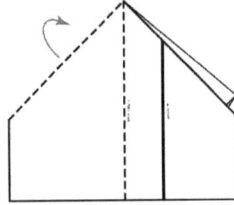 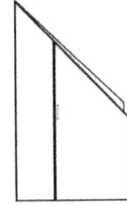 

Fold behind   Fold behind   Fold in the   Cut.
                                           middle.

Instructions: Follow the instructions to know how to cut and fold your worksheet and discover how Jesus died for you. Color and/or decorate your creation.

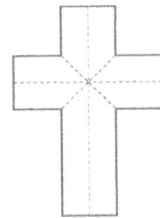

Finished
project
without
folding.

Fold Behind

Fold Behind

Fold in the middle

Cut

What
does it
mean
for us?

Celebrate the
resurrection!

Carefully cut out these two resurrection cards. Color them and decorate them as you like. Fold them as shown on the dotted line and you will notice that it seems that angels are flying. You can give these cards to your family or friends and tell them what the resurrection means for you.

What does it

mean for us?

¡Celebrate the
resurrection!

33

Jesus is
alive!

Jesus is
risen!

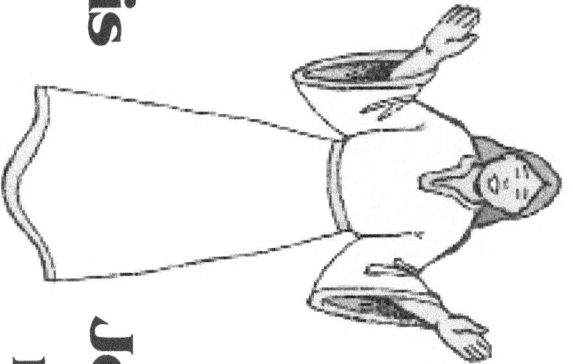

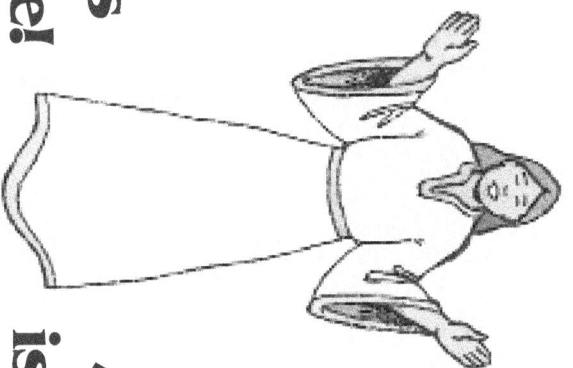

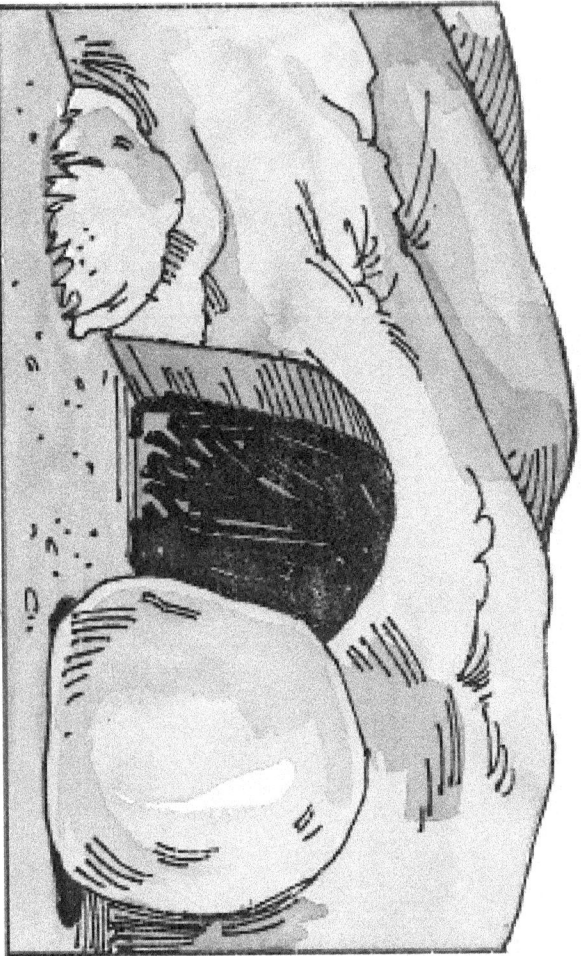

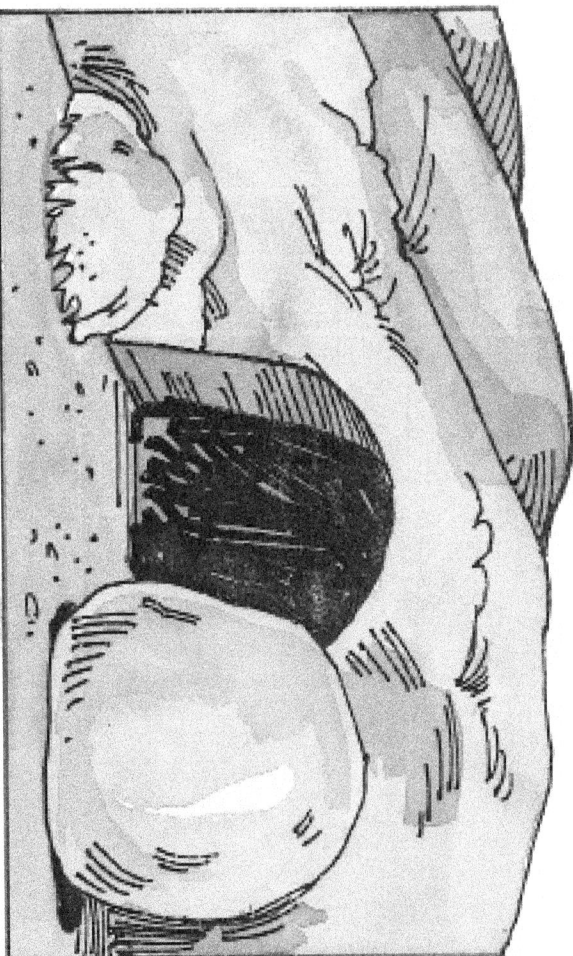

Jesus
is alive!

Jesus
is risen!

34

Who Said What ?

Twelve spies went into the promised land of Canaan. They all saw the same things, but they all had different interpretations of what they observed.

- How did the 10 spies feel?

- How did Joshua and Caleb feel?

Use these cards to remember the bible story. Imagine how the spies felt when they arrived in the land of Canaan. Do you think they were scared? Did Joshua and Caleb feel the same as the rest of the spies? What was the land of Canaan like? Who lived there? Show these cards to your family and tell them the Bible story you learned today.

You can be like Joshua and Caleb. Trust in God.

Cut here

"... the Lord is with us.
Do not be afraid of them!"
(Numbers 14:9)

Trust and Obey

Cut here

"Trust in the Lord with
all your heart."
(Proverbs 3:5a)

Instructions: Color and decorate these light switch covers. Read what each says. Carefully cut out the rectangle in the middle of each cover. Ask your parents or older siblings to help you stick them on light switches in your home. It could be in your room, in the hall, in the kitchen or in the bathroom. Now, every time you turn on or turn off the light remember that God is always with you. God gives you the strength to trust in him.

I trust in God.

cut here

God always keeps his word!

It isn't important what my friends do. I trust in God!

cut here

God gives me the strength to do what is right.

1

Cut Out Here

2

3

Instructions: Cut out the two circles. Then cut along the dark black line in each circle (so there will be a section to create an opening). Place the circle that has the text over the one that has the drawings, and join them with a brass fastener or clasp. Turn the lower circle to see the drawings through the opening you made. Discuss with your classmates what these drawings represent.

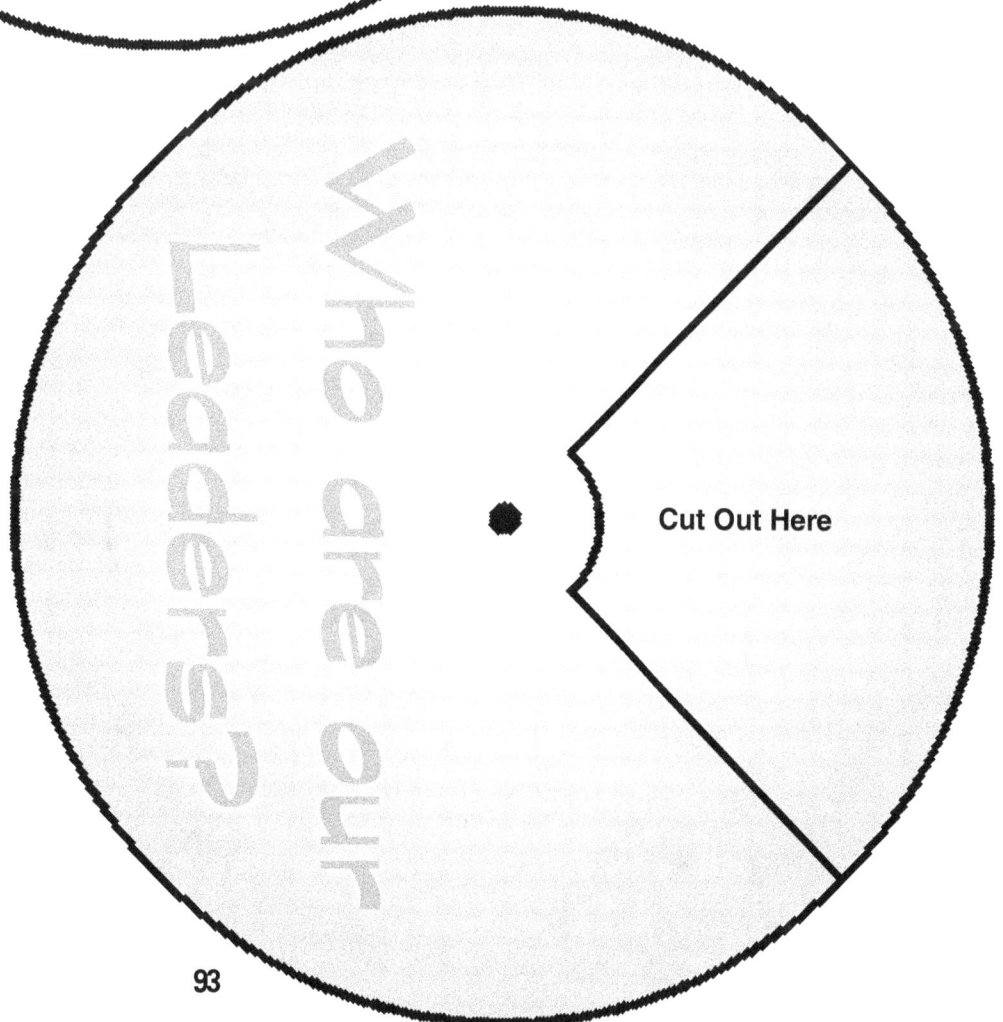

Who are our Leaders?

Cut Out Here

Crossing the Jordan River

"He did this so that all the peoples of the earth might know that the hand of the Lord is powerful and so that you might always fear the Lord you God".
(Joshua 4:24)

Slot A

Slot B

Cut the cartoon strip found on page 121 of your book. Fold as indicated on the dotted line. On this paper, make a cut on lines A and B, as indicated by the black line. On the back of your sheet, insert the cartoon strip on slot B, beginning from the box with the Ark of the Covenant, and insert it in slot A, so that they cross the river. Now you can gently pull the whole strip to see how the Israelites crossed the Jordan.

41

TRUST

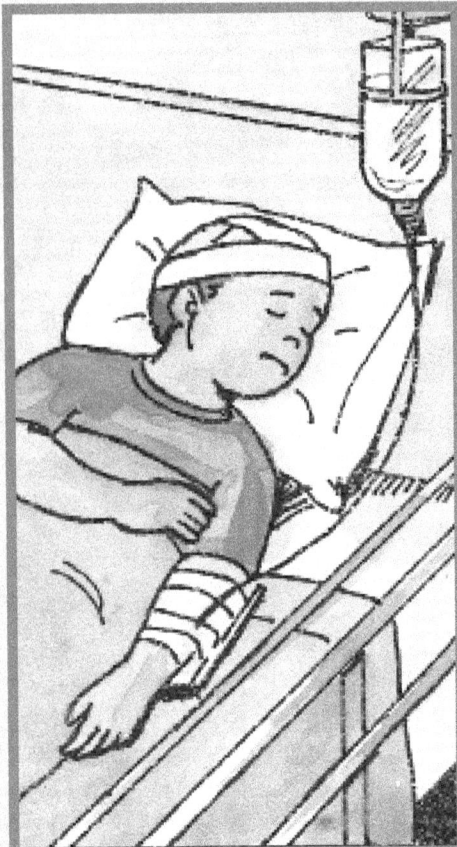

"Trust in the Lord with all your ♥, and lean not on your own understanding."

(Proverbs 3:5)

Explain what is happening in each picture. Talk with your class and decide in which situations you can trust in God. Read the verse that is in the middle of the drawings.

Mystery Puzzle?

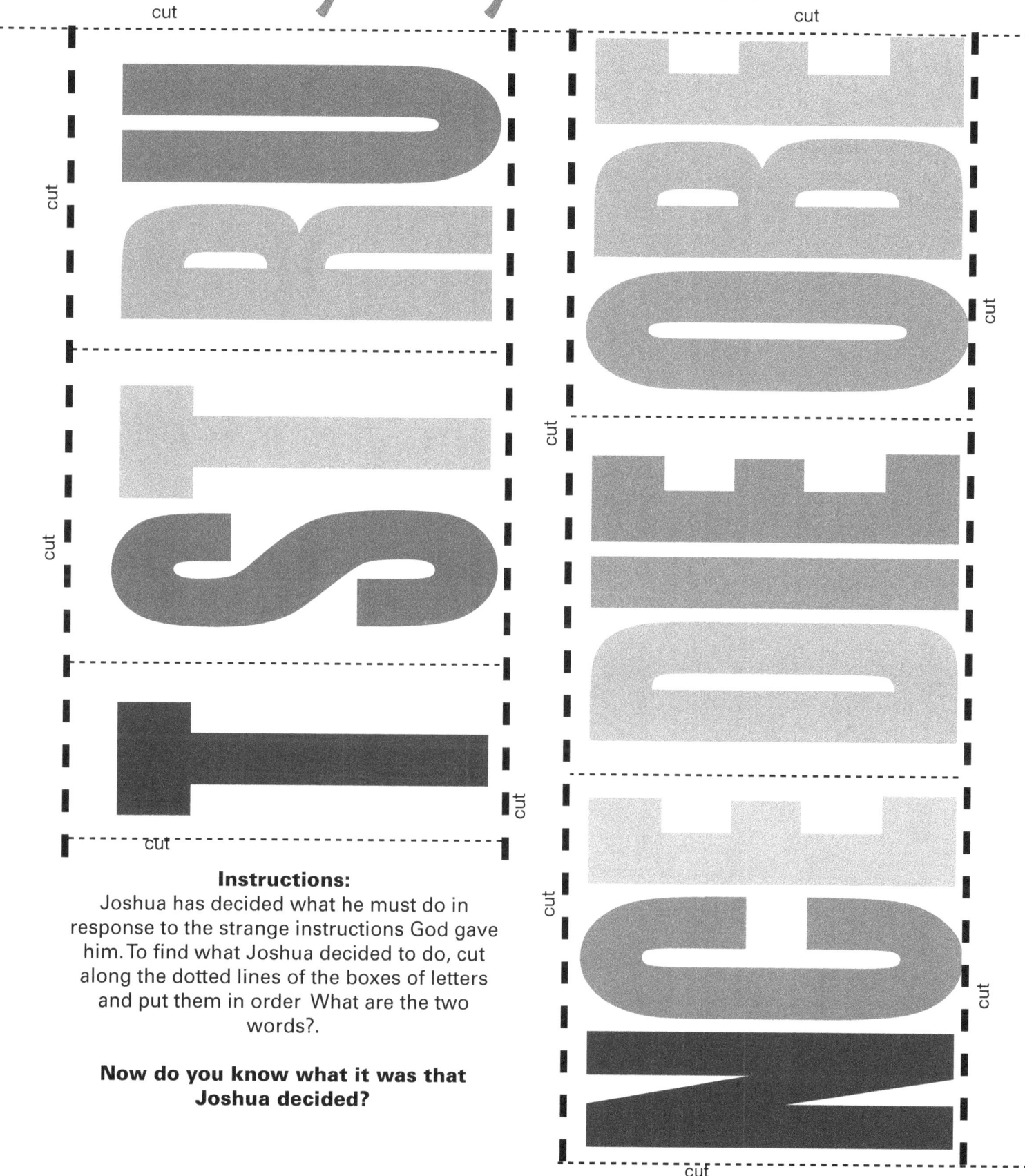

cut

cut

cut

cut

cut

cut

cut

cut

cut

cut

Instructions:
Joshua has decided what he must do in response to the strange instructions God gave him. To find what Joshua decided to do, cut along the dotted lines of the boxes of letters and put them in order What are the two words?.

Now do you know what it was that Joshua decided?

43

Door Hanger

Instructions: Cut out the door hanger. Put it on the handle of your door when you're praying.

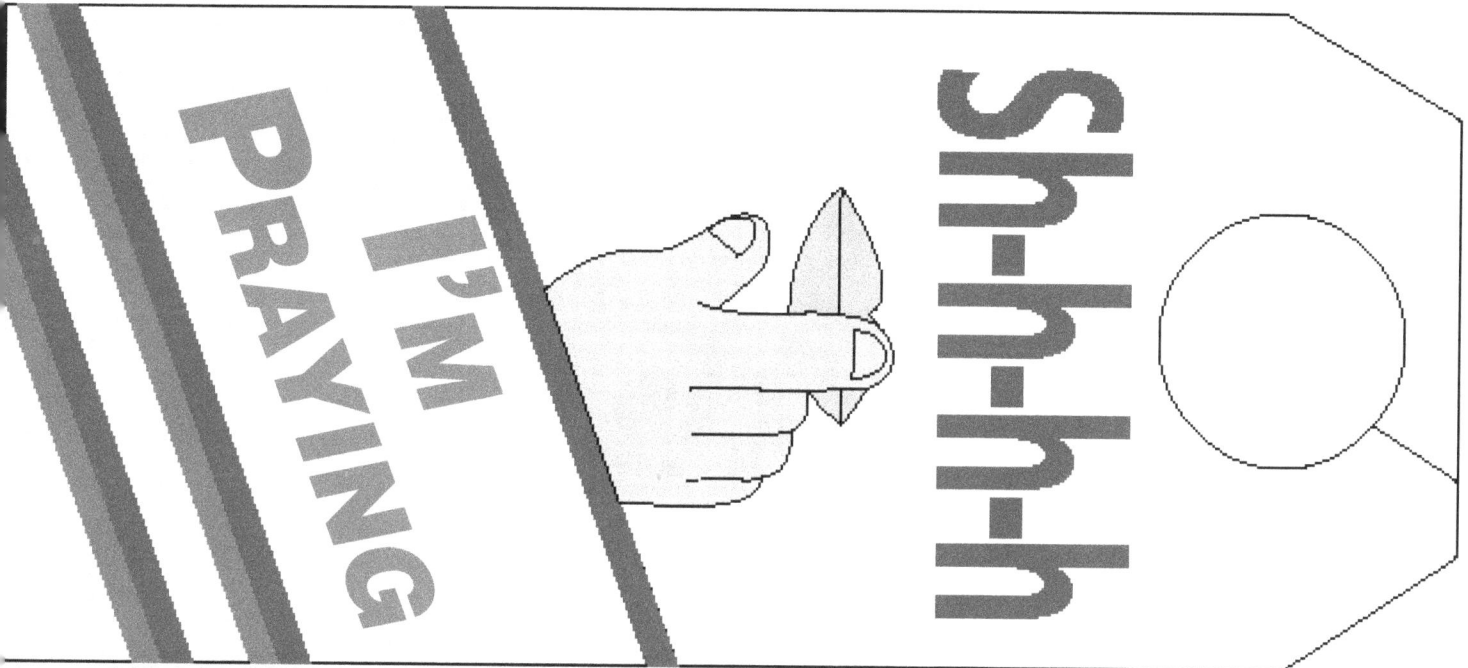

I'M PRAYING

Sh-h-h-h

YES, NO, WAIT

How do you think that God will answer your prayers? On the following stoplight drawings put a X on the red light if the answer is no, on the yellow if the answer is wait, or on the green if the answer is yes.

Please, God, allow my grandma to give me a lot of money for my birthday.

God, help my grandma to feel better.

God, please help me to be little like my little sister.

God, I feel very alone in this new school. Help me to make new friends.

God, help me to know what you want me to be when I grow.

God, Luis told a lie about me. Give me the strength to give him a strong punch.

GOD
LISTENS
TO MY
PRAYERS

Psalms 4:3

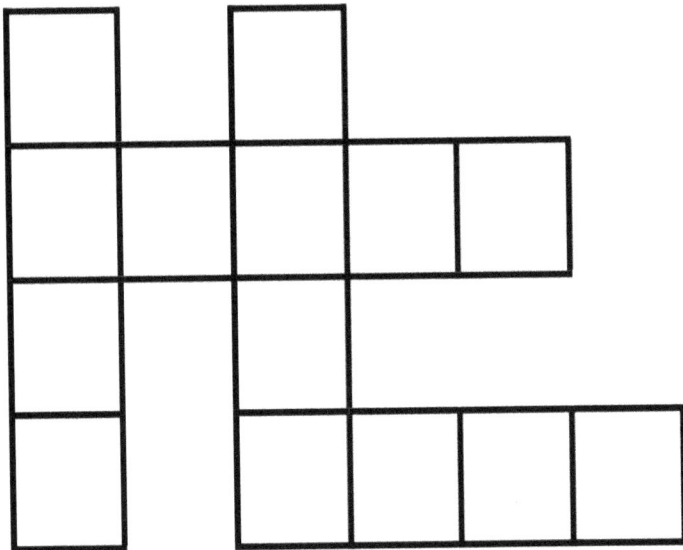

Words:

Lord
Hears
When
Call

The _____ _____ me

_____ I _____ to him.

(Psalms 4:3 paraphrased).

Instructions: First, use the words on the right to complete the crossword. Then use the words to complete the Bible verse.

TRUST IN GOD to DO IT RIGHT

Code: 1= a   2= c   3= d   4= e   5= g   6= h   7= i
8= m   9= n   10= r   11= s   12= t   13= u

$\overline{5}\ \overline{13}\ \overline{7}\ \overline{3}\ \overline{4}$ me

i $\overline{}$ your $\overline{12}\ \overline{10}$ u $\overline{12}\ \overline{6}$ me
$\overline{9}$

and $\overline{12}\ \overline{4}\ \overline{1}\ \overline{2}\ \overline{6}$ me .

PSALMS 25:5

Use the code to complete today's Bible verse.

47

Instructions: Look at the picture of Samuel and talk about ways that God speaks to people today. Read the Bible verse. Carefully cut along the solid black lines around the picture of Samuel and the Bible verse. Then fold the two boxes on the dotted lines (must stay in the form of a window). Tape a piece of paper on the back of your worksheet and draw a picture that shows how God speaks to you.

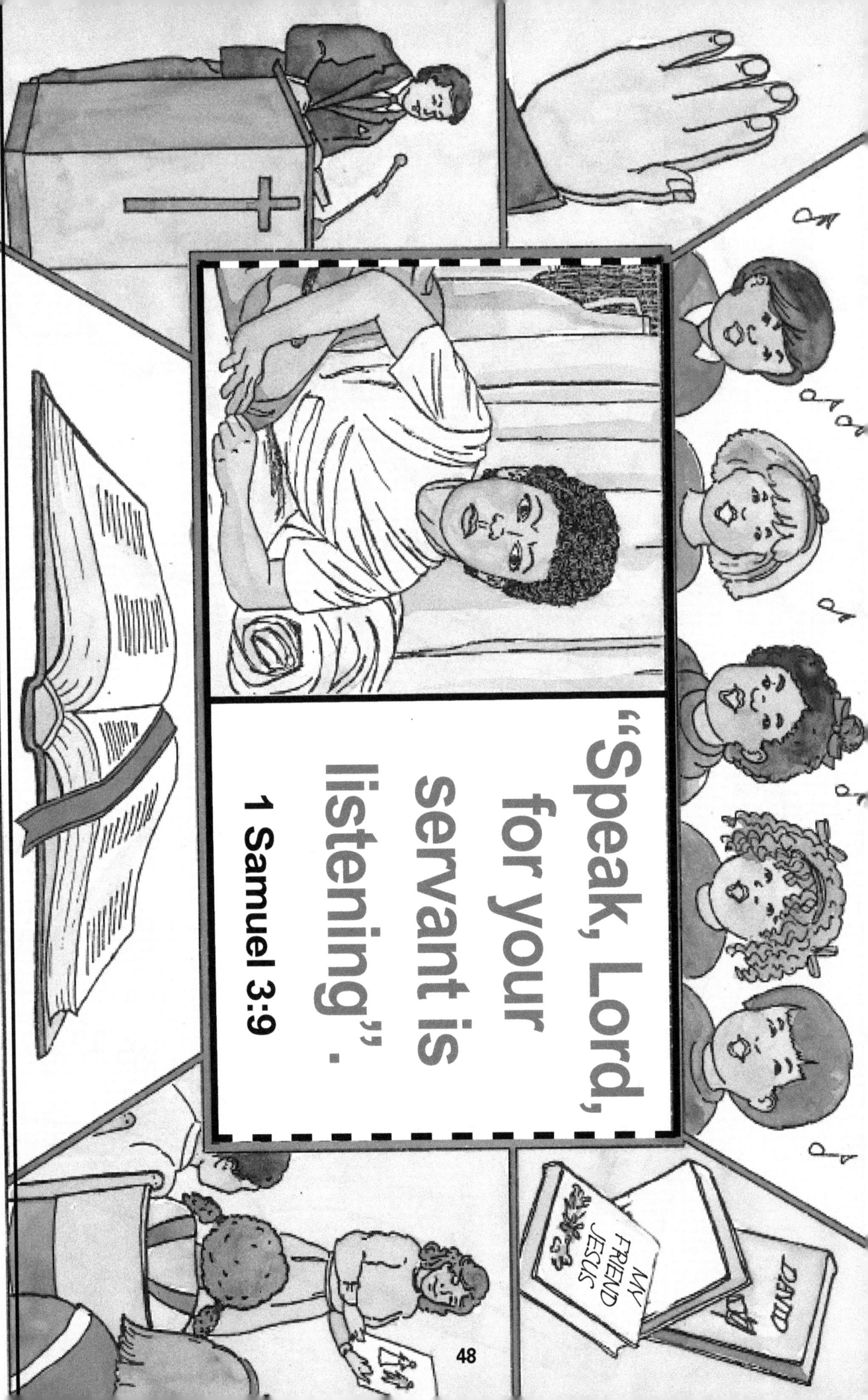

"Speak, Lord, for your servant is listening".

1 Samuel 3:9

48

Nehemiah Rebuilds the walls

1. Nehemiah was

2. He was sad because

3. Nehemiah asked the king to

4. This was not easy because

5. The walls were rebuilt quickly because

Cut out the blocks of stone from page 121 and 123 of your book. Find the one that corresponds to each of the sentences and paste it where it goes. Now you can read the whole story! Tell the story to your friends and family.

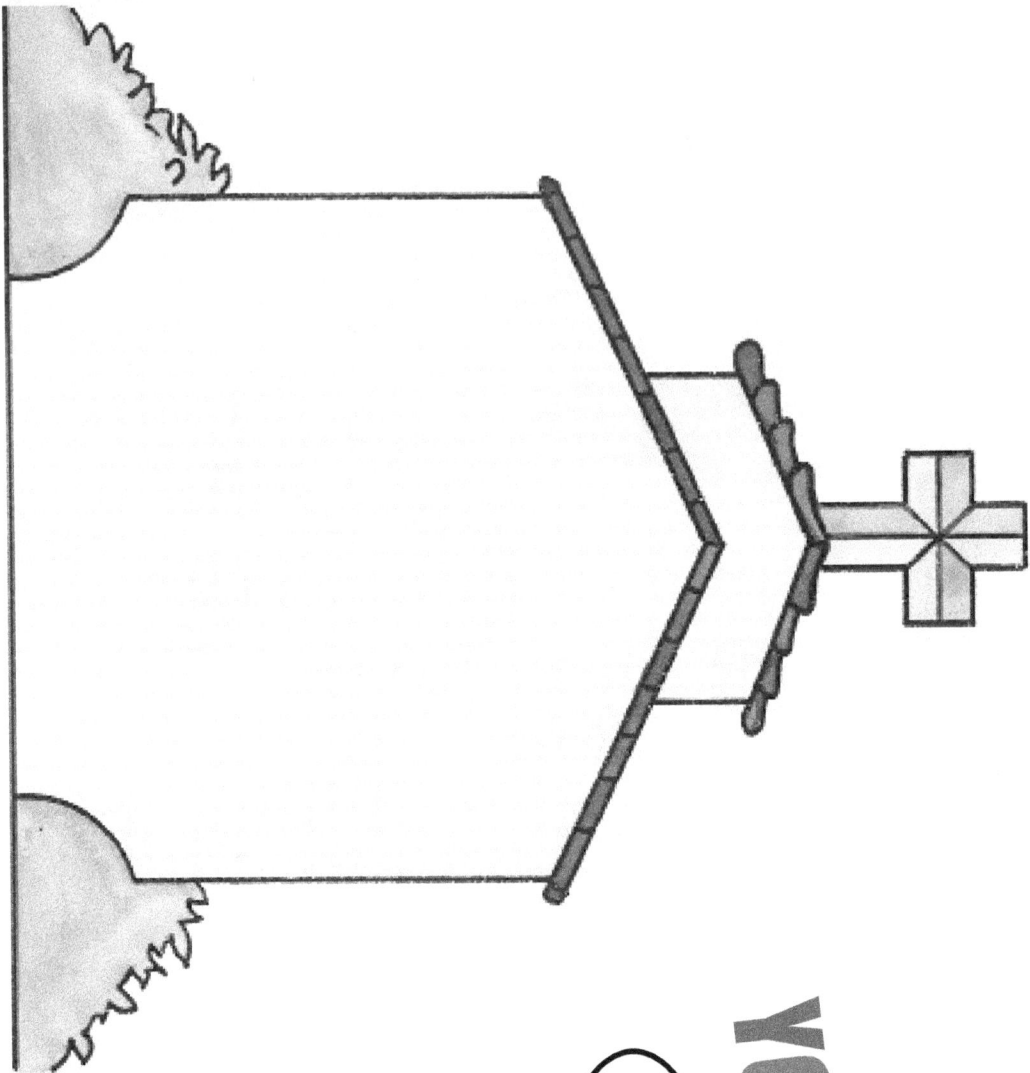

I can help do the work of God.

Cut out the two pieces on page 121. Paste them on to the church in the correct places for each figure, and read about the ways you can help carry out the work of God. In the shrubs you can write other ways in which you can be helpful.

YOU DECIDE!

Sometimes people try to keep us from doing the right thing. Read the following story and answer the questions with your classmates.

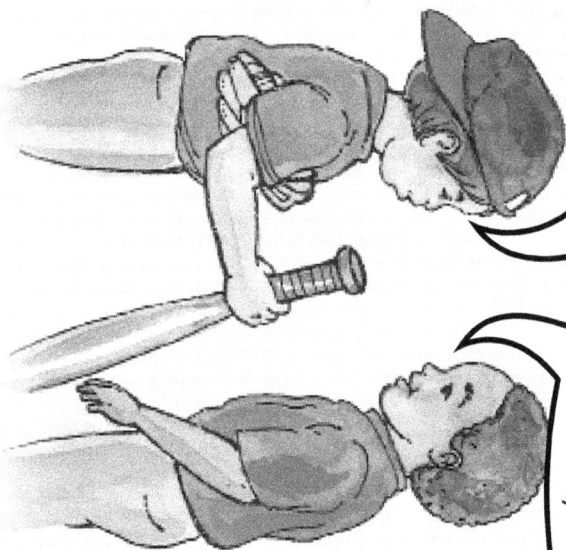

I would love to play with you, but I promised Ms. Anita that I would help her with her plants.

Let's play, Daniel! You can help her any other day.

1. Would it be wrong for Daniel to play with his friend? Why or why not?

2. Will it be easy or hard for Daniel to do the right thing? Why?

3. What can you do when someone tries to prevent you from doing the right thing?

50

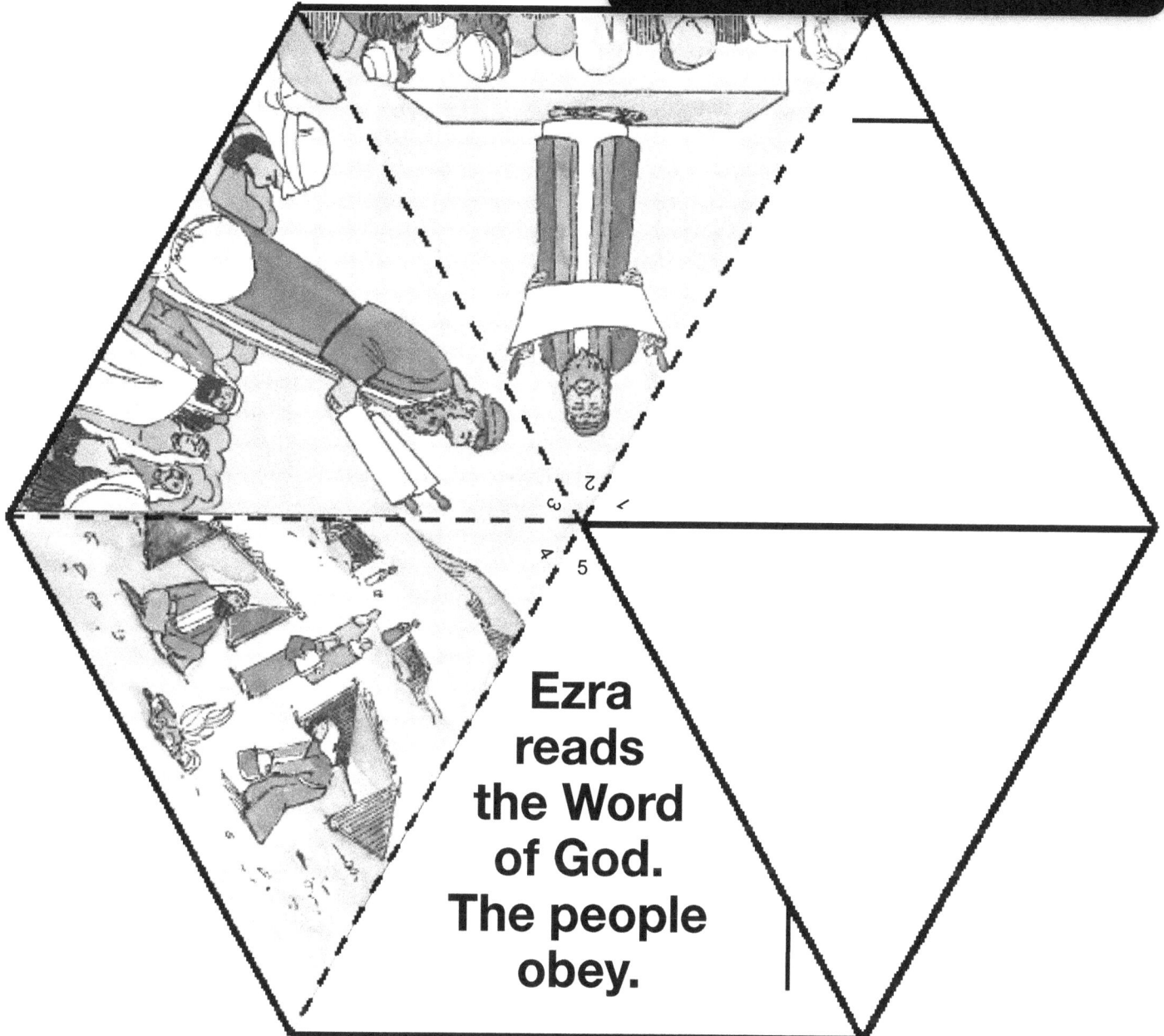

Ezra reads the Word of God. The people obey.

2 3 1 4 5

How to make history

Cut along the solid black lines. Carefully cut on the short solid black lines (slits) found in triangle 1 and 5. Fold along the dotted lines. Place the slit in triangle 5 into the slit in triangle 1. Use this activity to retell the Bible story we learned today. Tell about what the people did when they heard the Word of God.

You can turn the activity sheet over and put it together so the other side shows. Talk with your friends about how you can hear and obey the word of God everyday.

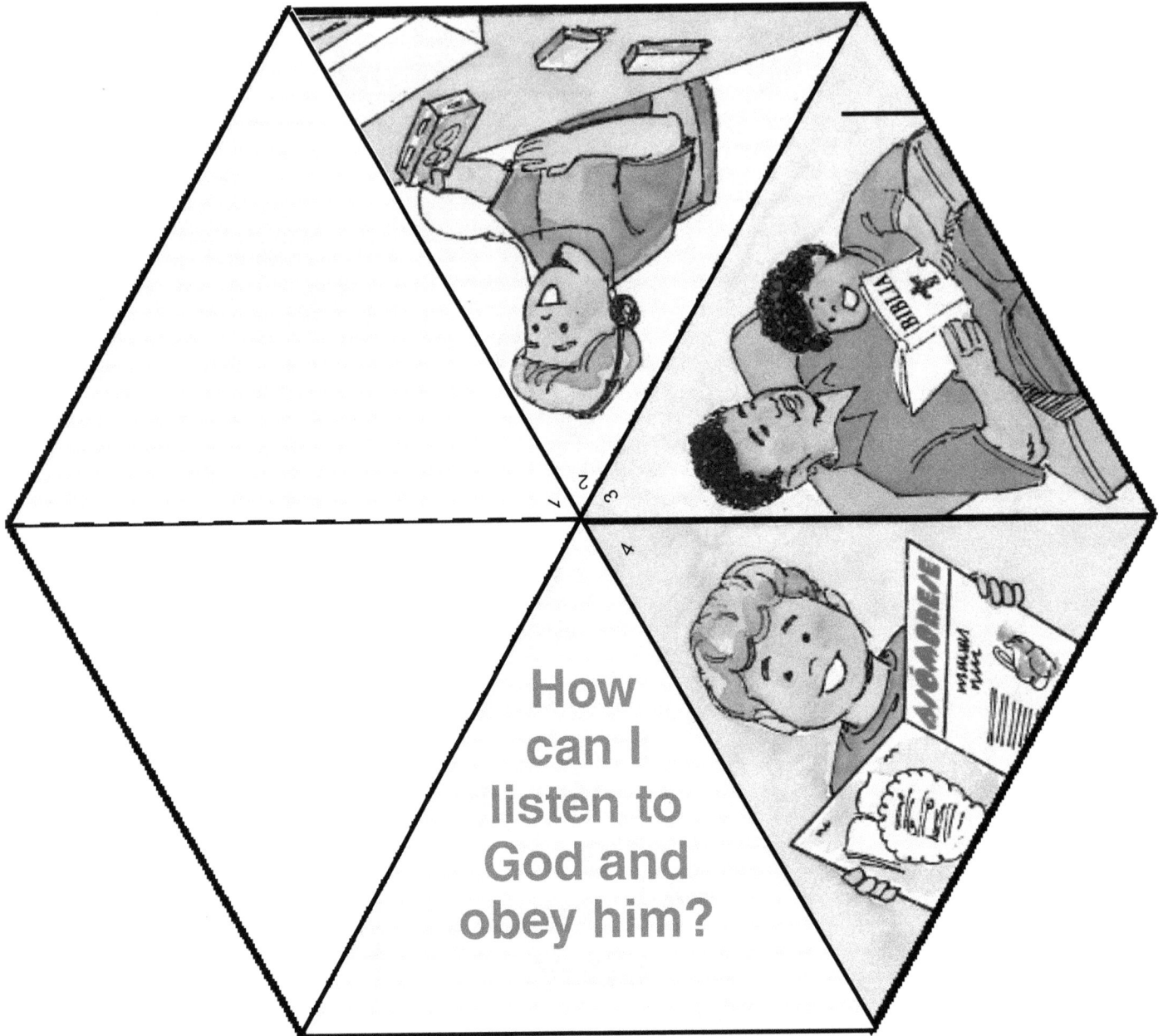

How
can I
listen to
God and
obey him?

God Created the Seasons

The seasons of the year are: Spring, Summer, Autumn and Winter.

Cut out the four children and the four names of the seasons that are on page 129. Place the pictures of the children in the correct picture. Then glue them on the activity sheet. Glue the names of the seasons at the bottom of the correct picture.

God Created

M	S	U	S	S	S	D	S	H	P
N	T	E	J	☆	M	U	O	N
E	A	R	T	H	T	N	M	I
H	R	D	G	K	E	L	Q	G
H	E	A	V	E	N	S	C	H
J	P	Y	B	M	O	O	N	T
M	L	I	G	H	T	K	Y	U

Word Bank:

moon star heavens sun
night **day** **light** earth

Can you find these words in the letter soup? When you find a word, color each letter of that word with the same color (for example: color all the letters of the word "sun" yellow.) If you find all 8 words, color in the star.

54

Plants and Animals Help Us

What do you think happens first? Look at the rows of pictures. In each row, at the bottom of each picture in the small square, write the number 1 for the picture that shows what happens first, a 2 for the what happens second and a 3 for what happens last.

Key:

d	i	o	s	e	h	c	a	b	r	l	n	t	q	u
1	2	3	4	5	6	7	8	9	10	11	12	13	14	15

Use the code to find the lost letters. Write the letters on the blank lines. You can look for the verse in your Bible if you need help.

"H_w   ma_y   a_e
   3   12   10

y_u_   w_ _ks,   L_r_!
 3 10   3 10   3 1

l_   w_ _d_m
12   2 4 3

yo_   m_ _e   t_ _m   _ _ _;
15   8 1   6 5   8 11 11

t_e   ear_ _   i_   fu_ _
 6   13 6   4   11 11

_f   y_ _r   _rea_ure_.
3   3 15   7   13   4

Psalms 104:24

Thank You, God!

What plants and animals would you thank God for?
Write the names of two plants and two animals you thank God for.

_____   _____

_____   _____

God's Special Creation

How much of the Bible story do you remember? Draw a happy face in the circle by the sentences that are true and a sad face by the ones that are false.

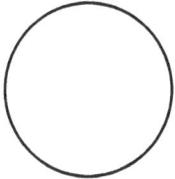

○ God created people first.

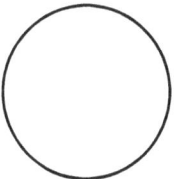

○ God told the animals to name the plants.

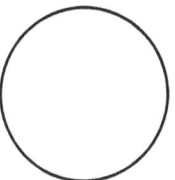

○ God gave people the task of caring for the plants and animals.

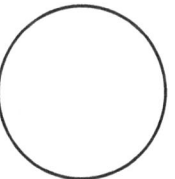

○ God was pleased with the man and woman he had created.

Genesis 1:27

Some of the words of the Bible verse are out of place.
Draw a line from the word to the place in the verse that it belongs.

mankind   God   image

So _____ created _____ in his own _____, in

female   the image of God he _____ them; created

_____ and _____ he created them.

male   (Genesis 1:27)

Different
but
the same

Look at the pictures and answer the questions:

1. How are these children the same? How are they different?

2. Which of these children were created by God?

3. Who does God love the most?

4. Who do you think God wants you to show love to?

My Friend and I

God created people, but we are not all the same. Work with your friends on this part of the activity. In the spaces below write how you and your friend are alike or different.

1. My friend's name is _____.

2. My friend has _____ colored eyes and his/her hair is _____.

3. My friend is in the _____ grade.

4. My friend's favorite food is _____.

5. What my friend likes most about Sunday School is _____

_____.

1. My name is _____.

2. My eye color is _____ and my hair is_____ .

3. I am in the _____ grade.

4. My favorite food is _____.

5. What I like most about Sunday School is _____

_____.

God cares for the world

God created our world. He also cares for you. To find some of the ways that He cares for you, write the name of the pictures on the lines.

1. God sends  _____ and _____ to make the trees and flowers will grow .

2. The plants produce  _____ that grow and become new plants.

3. Mothers have _____ that grow up and then have their own children.

4. God give us _____ to eat.

5. God gives us our _____ and    _____ .

59

God thinks of everything

"As long as the earth endures, seedtime and harvest, cold and heat, summer and winter, day and night, will never cease." (Genesis 8:22).

God cares for the world He created. He knows exactly what plants and animals need. Color the picture. Write a prayer of thanks to God because He cares for our world and he cares for you!

Thank you, God, _____

_____

_____

I Can Help

START

I walked on the neighbors grass.

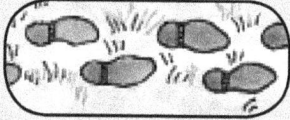

Go back 1 space.

I threw a candy wrapper on the ground.

Go back 1 space.

I wasted water.

Lose 1 turn.

I helped to plant a tree.

Go forward 1 space.

I put my trash in the trash can.

Get 1 extra turn.

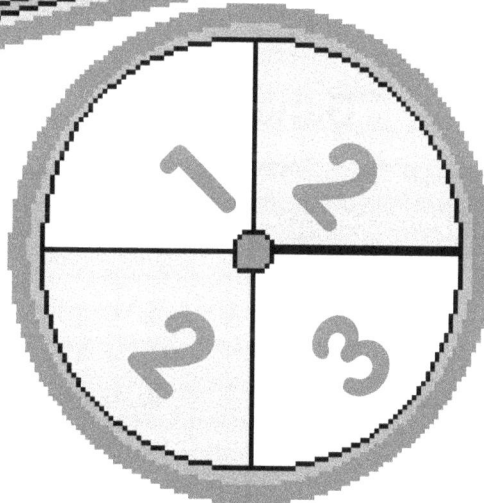

"In the beginning God created the heavens and the earth."

(Genesis 1:1).

I watered the plants.

Go forward 3 spaces.

I ran through the flowerbed.

Go back 1 space..

I fed the birds.

Go ahead 1 space.

Find game pieces for the game, you can use coins or seeds. Carefully cut out the circle with the numbers (you can put a paper clip in the middle to make it spin). Two players can participate or form teams. Take turns spinning the circle and move your game piece according to the number that comes up. Follow the instructions in each box. The first player or team to reach the Bible verse - Genesis 1:1 - is the winner.

God is the Creator!

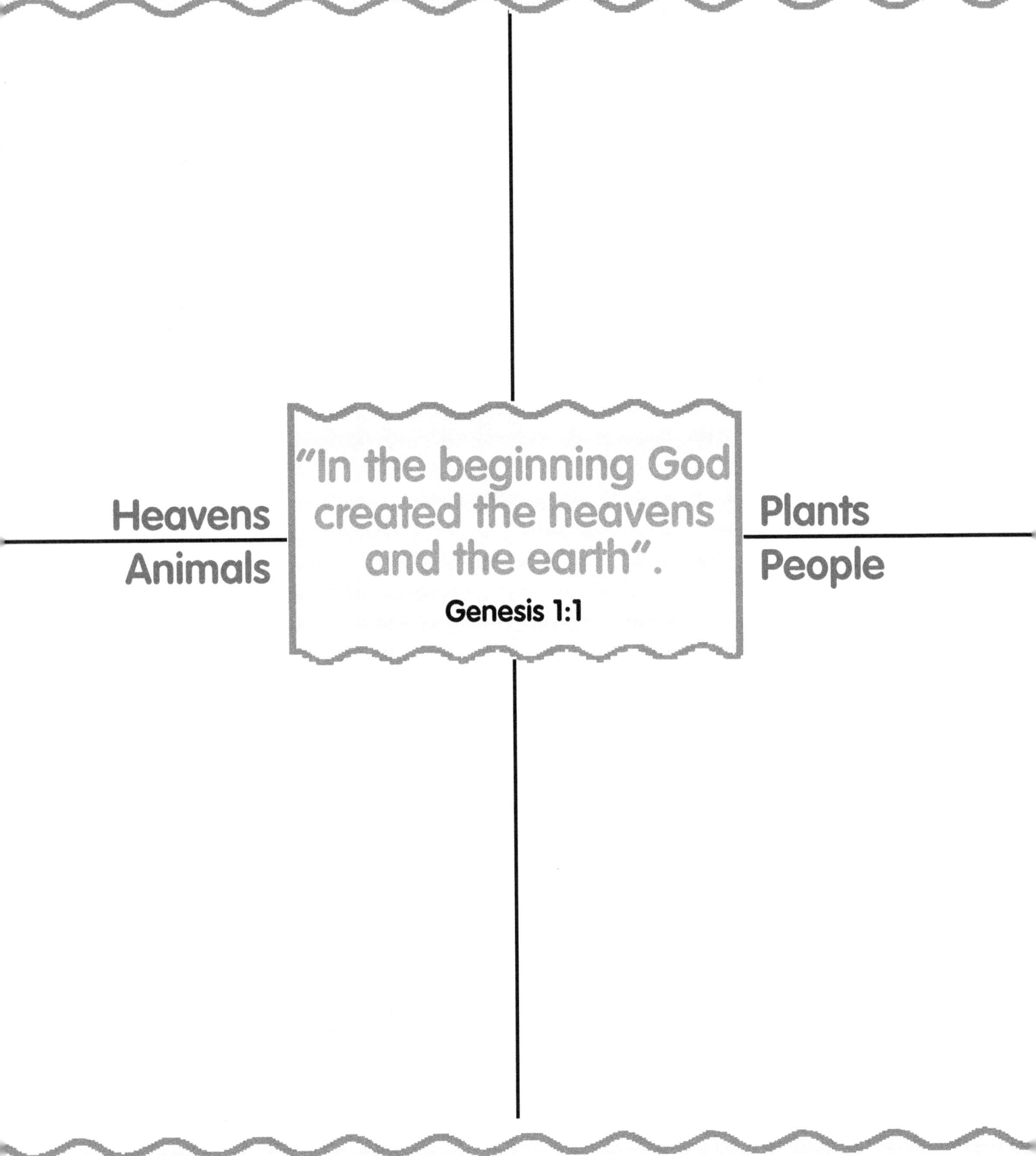

Heavens

Animals

"In the beginning God created the heavens and the earth".

Genesis 1:1

Plants

People

In each square, draw a picture of something God created according to the Bible verse.

Who is following Jesus?

I like what he says.

Listen to him, he's telling the truth!

I cannot believe him.

I am going to do what he says.

This is wrong.

I believe in him.

I believe in him.

Color the people who are following Jesus.

What will they do?

Look at the illustration. What do you think happened? Make up a story about what you think is happening in this picture. Then draw or write down what you imagine most children would do or say in the same situation. Then, next to the bottom picture, explain what you think would happen if the children were followers of Jesus.

Are you a follower of Jesus? How would you react?

Who is Jesus?

Color the dialogue balloons of people who know something about Jesus. Make a star on the balloon that has the best answer. Then write the best answer on the lines below.

A man from the Bible.

A teacher.

I don't know.

The son of God.

Someone who lived a long time ago.

Jesus is _____

_____

_____ .

Jesus shows that he is the Son of God

1.

Make a cut along solid black lines numbered 1 and 2 on this page. Cut out the figure of Jairus's daughter, the strips with the dove and the words of God found on page 129. Fold back the tabs at the ends, at the base of the strips (marked by dotted lines). Insert the strips by the bending part into the openings of the activity sheet. Then unfold the fins so that the strip does not leave its place. Strip 1 corresponds to the baptism of Jesus and the second to the scene on the mountain. Now you can move it up and down. With a pin or clasp, place the figure of Jairus's daughter in the second painting. You can lay her down and then have her stand up to remember the Bible story and tell it to others.

2.

Searching for Kind People

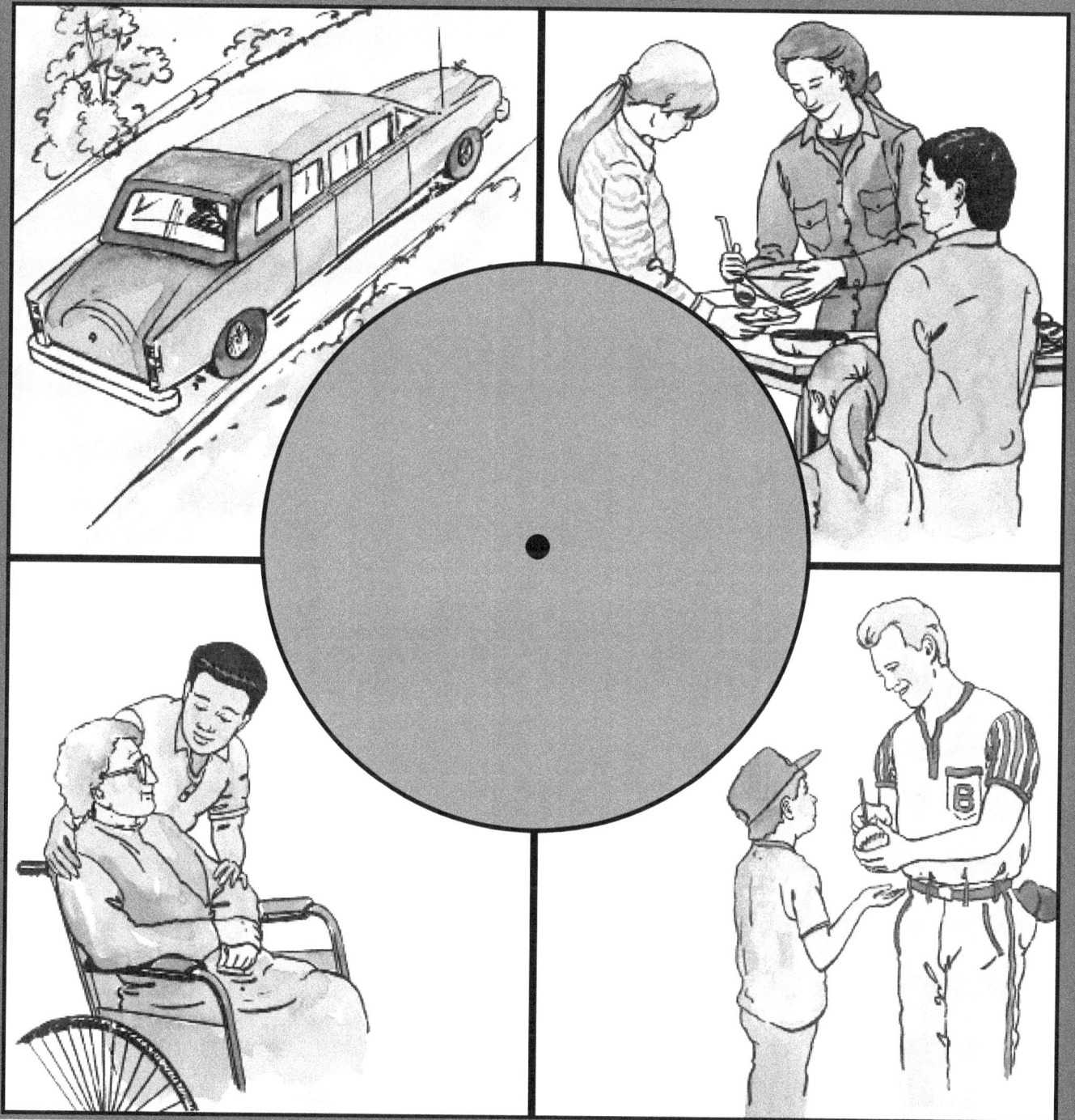

Cut out the searchlight figure on page 131, and place it in the center of the circle with a paper clip or clasp. Move the searchlight to point to each drawing. Do you think the people in the drawings are kind? Why or why not?

If you want to be nice...

cut here

cut here

Instructions:
Cut out the two large circles and the two small ovals in the speech bubbles in the top circle. Place the circles, one on top of the other, putting the one with the picture on the top. Connect the circles with a metal brad so they can turn. Turn the circle on the bottom to change the word bubbles and tell the story.

We wish for
Honor

Be a Server

You must serve

Do you want
to be like me?

We want to be kind

Can I be first?

Jesus shows his love

What is needed to complete this drawing?
Finish it and color it. Can you tell how
Jesus showed love to his friends?

71

John 21:16

Again ☐ said, " ☐ son of John, do you ☐ me?

He answered: Yes, Lord; you know that I ☐ you.

☐ said: Take care of my ☐ ".

Cut out the figures on page 131 and paste them into the spaces that correspond to them in the verse.

Sleepy

Just

Faithful

Without Sin

Powerful

Sinner

Weak

Pure

Instructions: Cut out the pieces of the puzzle. Choose those that describe God. Tape the pieces to make a square. Turn the puzzle over to find a secret message.

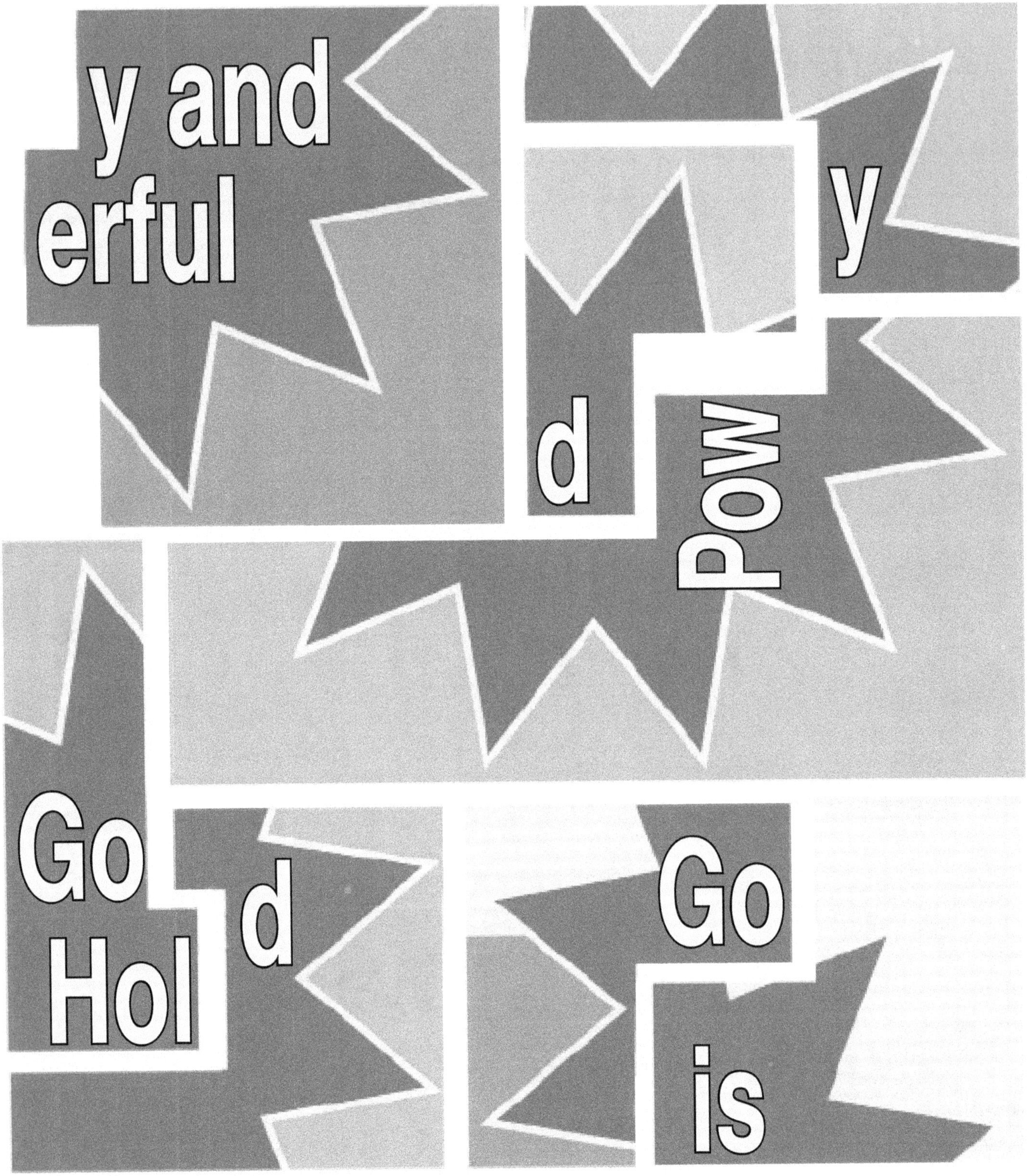

y and
erful

y

d

Pow

Go
Hol d

Go

is

What do these people deserve?

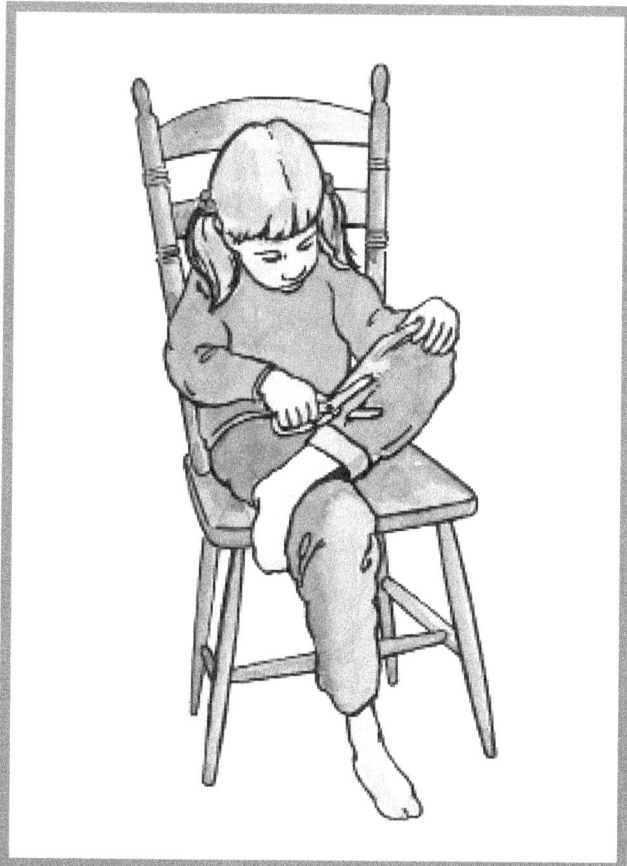

Faithful

God is

Welcome to the Family of God
"Yet to all who did receive him, to those who believed in his name, he gave the right to become children of God-" (John 1:12).

4 Ask

4. Ask God to forgive you.

1 John 1:9

3 Repent

3. Repent of your sins.

Romans 6:23

2 Believe

2. Believe that Jesus died for you.

Romans 5:8

1 Recognize

1. Recognize that you are a sinner.

Romans 3:23

Color the phrase: "God is Faithful". Fold the sheet on the dotted lines to form a ladder. First fold step 1 backwards and step 2 forward, then repeat the procedure with the other steps. Discuss with your classmates and your teacher the steps you must take to become a child of God.

Psalm 86:5

The
Loving
Father

1

you

2

to

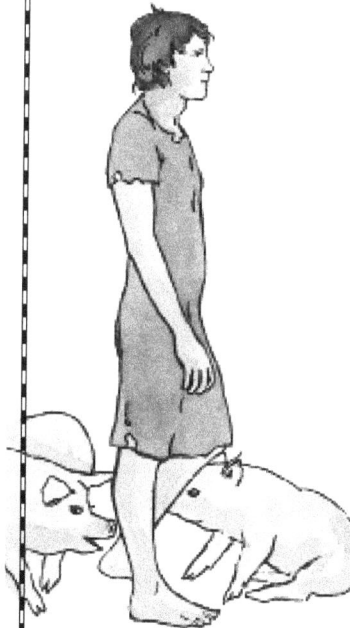

3

call

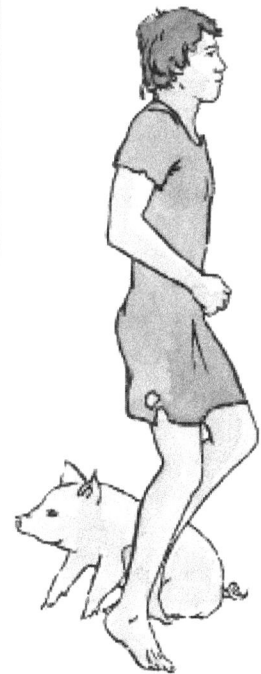

4

Instructions: Use these pages (77-80) to put together a moving book about a loving parent. Cut out the instruction strips and cards along the black lines. Match them in order of 1 to 8. Fold them along the dotted lines, so that you have 16 pages left. Join them along the fold.

Lord,

15

You,

16

forgiving

13

are

14

who

5

all

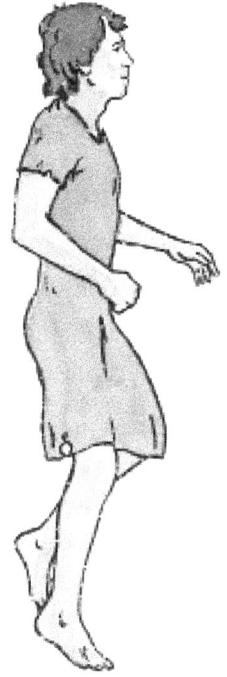

6

to

7

love

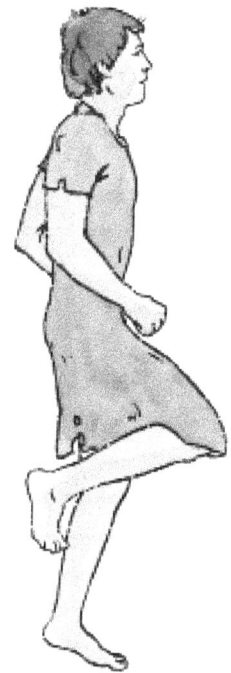

8

Cut along the solid black lines.

good,

11

and

12

in

9

abounding

10

3 IN 1

Wife

Mother

Grandmother

Father

God

Son

Holy Spirit

Father

God

Son

Holy Spirit

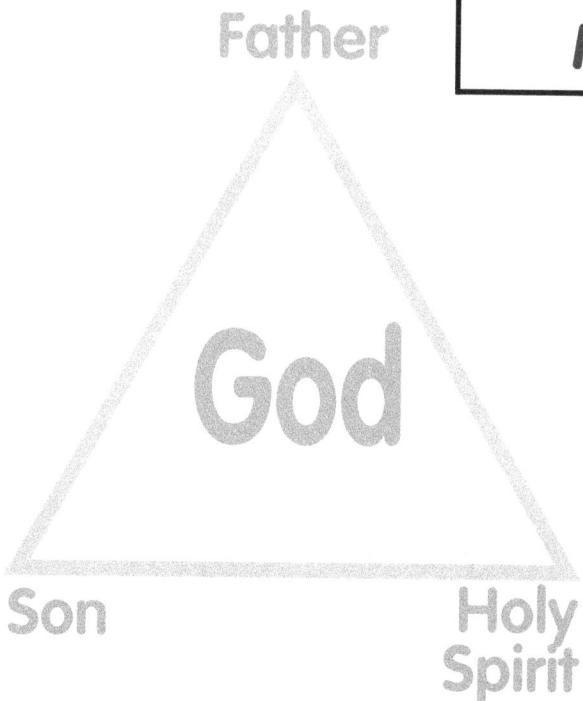

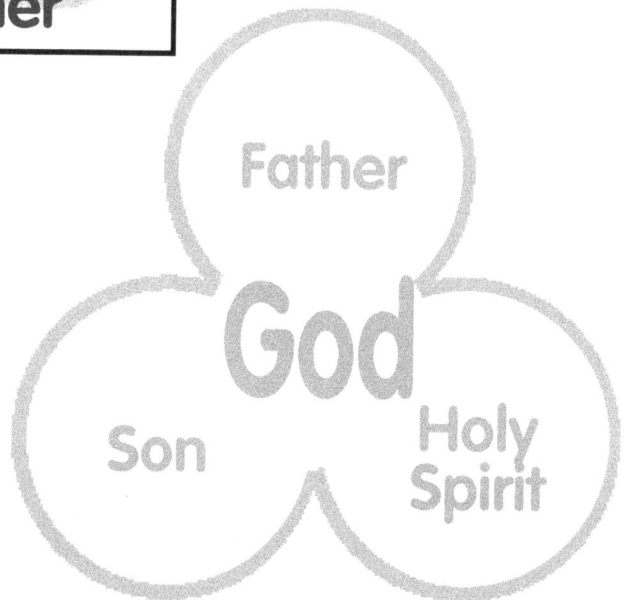

Use these illustrations to talk about the Trinity.

"And I will ask the Father, and he will give you another advocate to help you and be with you forever".

John 14:16

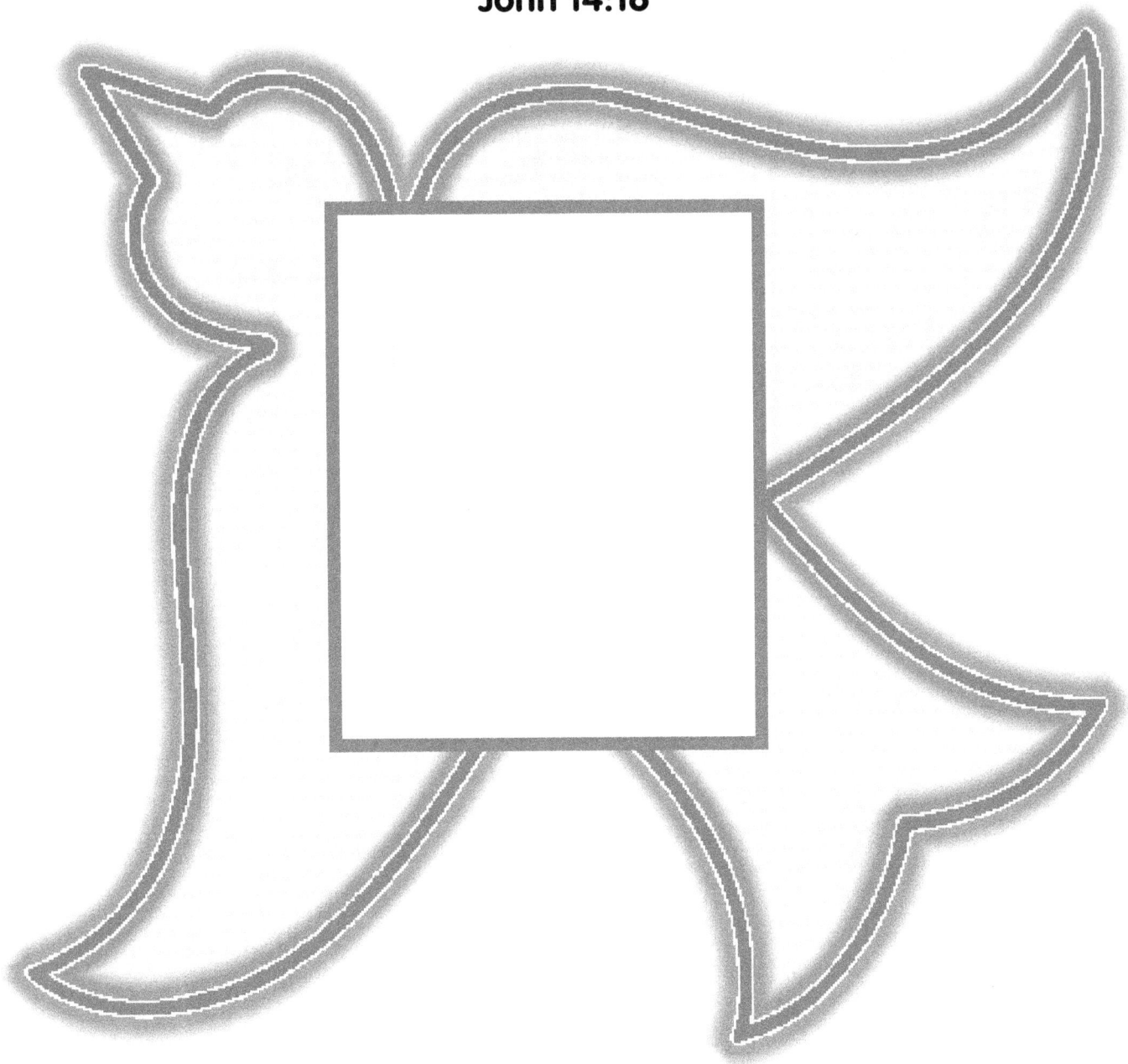

The Holy Spirit is always with

_____.

Finish this small poster that helps remind you that the Holy Spirit is always with you. Draw or paste a photograph of yourself in the space provided. Write your name on the line.

1.

2.

Vote for the King

Vote for the King		
My Vote	1	2
God's Vote	1	2

Imagine that you live in Bible times and you have to vote to choose a new king. Make a check mark in the box that represents the person you chose.

What do you see?

Cut out the eight cards below. Place them with the words "what God sees" and "what people see" face up. Mix them together. Then raise a card that says "what people see" so that the picture on the back shows and ask "What do people see"?, and describe what you think the person in the picture is like. Now turn over one of the cards that says "what God sees" and read what God thinks about that same person. Do the same with the rest of the cards. You can play as many times as you want. Have fun!

What God Sees	What God Sees	What People See	What People See
What God Sees	**What God Sees**	**What People See**	**What People See**

1 Samuel 16:7b

 **The Lord**

 **does not look at**

 **the things people look at,**

 **People**

 **look at**

 **the outward appearance,**

but the Lord

 **looks**

at the heart.

Memorize this verse.

loving   friendly

liar   cheater

David trusts in God

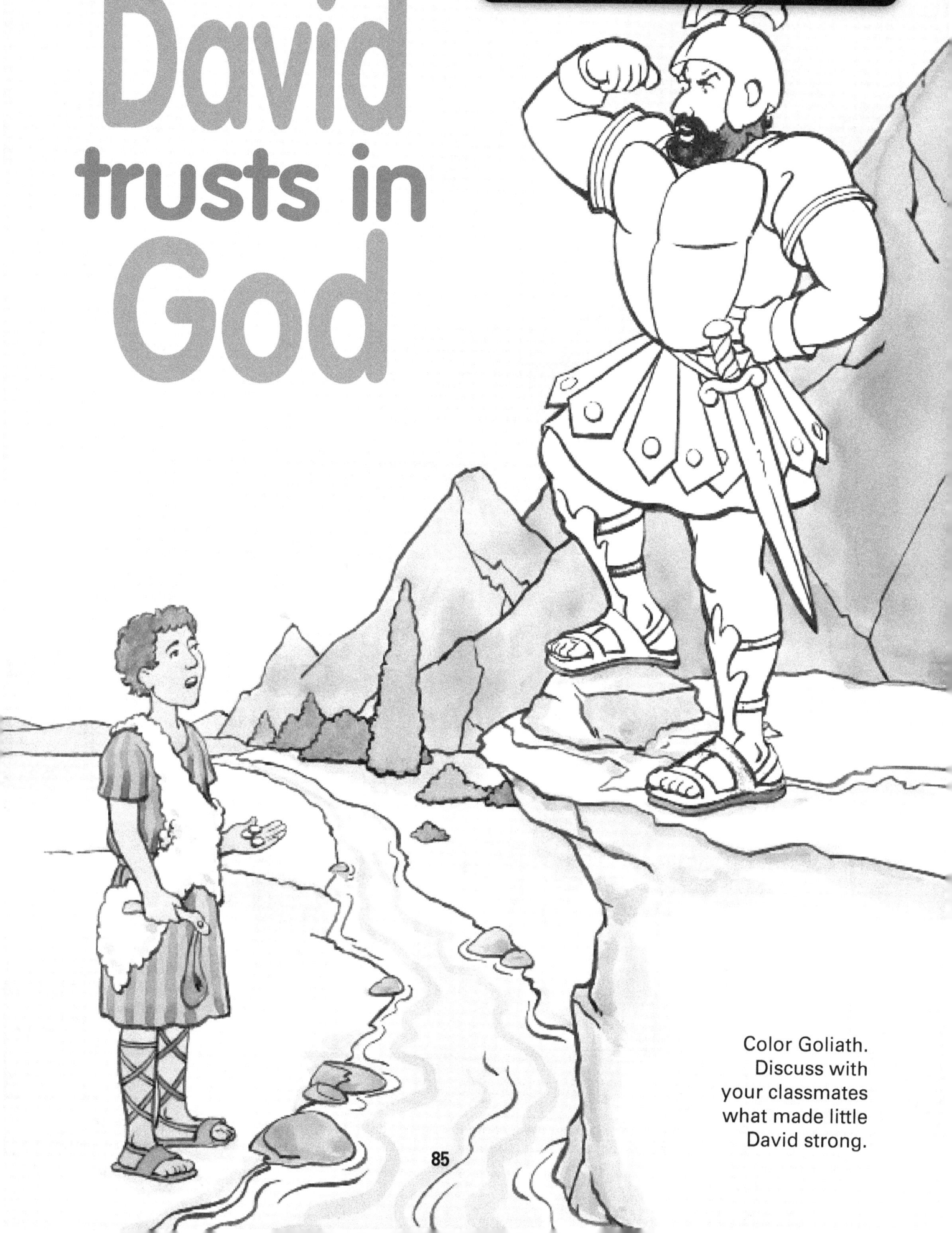

Color Goliath. Discuss with your classmates what made little David strong.

God is Bigger
than any person or problem.

Trust in God

A Reminder of Trust
Fold this strip back along the dotted line. Fold the sheet along the middle dotted line so that your confidence reminder can stand. Write your name on the line and decorate your reminder as you like. In the blank space draw something that shows you how to trust in God.

Who is a good friend?

¿Which of these children would you choose to be your friend? Color the picture and then tell the class who you would like to be your friend.

A story of friendship

Sebastian loves God. Draw a picture below showing how Sebastian can show love to his friend Antonio.

> Let's play in the pond!

Danger!

Let's Chose our Friends

Here are four good ideas about how you can choose your friends. Fill in the blank spaces with the correct word. Can you think of any other ideas of how you can choose your friends?

wisdom **appreciate** **do** **God**

1. Choose friends who like to _____ the same things as you do.

2. Choose friends who love _____ and try to do the right thing.

3. Choose friends that _____ you and that like to be with you.

4. Ask God to help you use _____ to choose your friends.

88

David

shows
mercy

Cut our the strip on page 127 for use with this Lesson. Cut along the two solid black lines so you can insert the strip with David's hand, the arrow, and the piece of fabric.

What Happens Next?

Look at all of the drawings. What is happening? Draw a picture of that you think happens next.

The Promise of a Friend

"I'll give you everything that your grandfather had." David kept his promise.

8 | 1
6 | 3

David and Jonathan promise to always be friends.

David became King. And he asked himself: "How shall I fulfill the promise that I made to Jonathan?"

Cut out this page along the solid black lines. Fold on the dotted lines. Now make a booklet by placing the pages in order from 1 to 8. Join your pages along the folded part. Show your booklet to your friends and family. Tell them how David kept his promise to Jonathan.

David and Jonathan were friends.

"Bring me the son of Jonathan", said David.

2 7
4 5

Jonathan cared for David when he was in trouble.

Obedience Reminder:

I want to obey!

CHICO

3

Obedience Reminder:

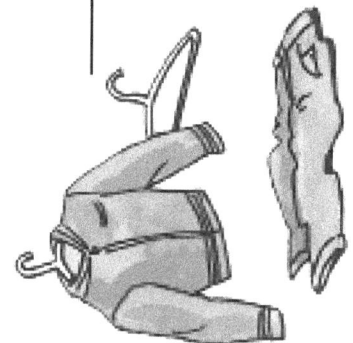

I want to obey!

CHICO

4

1

Obedience Reminder:

I want to obey!

CHICO

2

Obedience Reminder:

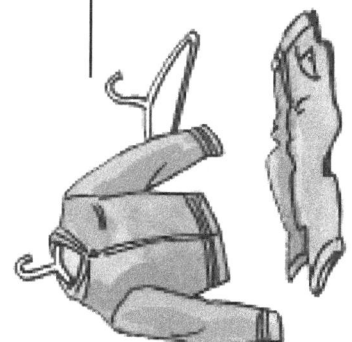

I want to obey!

CHICO

Instructions: Cut out the "Obedience Reminder" cards along the black lines. Decorate an envelope, put the cards in the envelope and give it to your parents. Together with your parents, decide what should go on these reminders. Use these reminder cards to honor and obey your parents.

Children, obey
your parents in
everything, for this
pleases the Lord.

(Colossians 3:20).

Honor your father
and your mother...

(Exodus 20:12).

Dear Parents:
These cards will help your children remember that obedience is very
important. Talk to them about times when they have difficulty obeying,
and encourage them to follow God's commandments about obedient
behavior. Choose four activities in which your child has a hard time
with obedience, and use these cards to help them remember what they
learned in this Bible class. Let them read the verse on the card and
reflect on their behavior.
It is very important that you pray with your child(ren) and encourage
them to be obedient.

Children, obey your
parents in the Lord, for
this is right.

(Ephesians 6:1)

Honor your father and
your mother, as the
Lord your God has
commanded you, so that
you may live long and
that it may go well with
you in the land the Lord
your God is giving you.

(Deuteronomy 5:16).

94

The stormed is calmed

One day there was a terrible storm while Jesus and his disciples were in a boat. The disciples were very worried, but Jesus calmed the storm and told his friends that they had to trust him.

Fold this sheet on the dotted line. Very carefully, cut the small black lines to make ten openings. Now unfold the sheet Then cut out the "trust" strip on page 125.

Insert the strip through the openings you made. Start from the right side by inserting the strip underneath the drawing. Slide the strip to show the stormy waves or to calm them. We can "trust" in God.

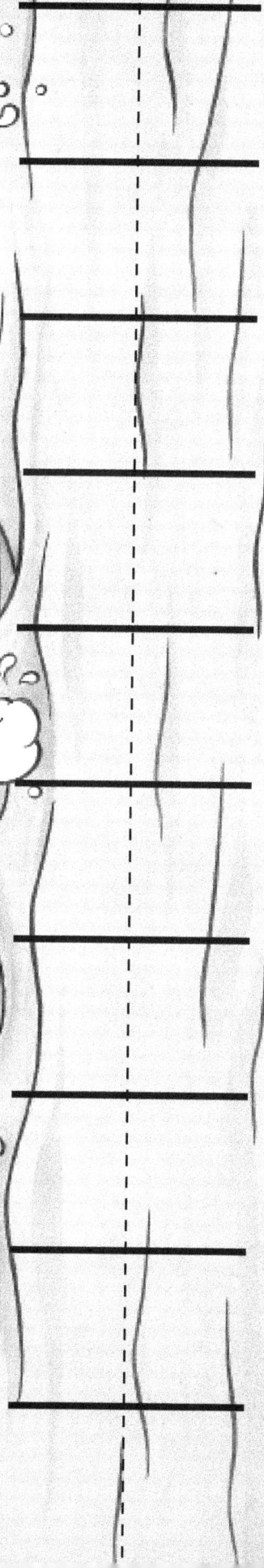

Hidden Message

```
S M O W I L E J N
H G U J I K L S O
P G Y O T G W D Q
T O R V U B S Z T
K O N F I Y A N S
O E I C G F N M S
P N L O A E R N A
K J G H O M D V S
B P W I T D G Y E
```

Choose your favorite color and color the letters that have a
dot on them to find the hidden message.

When I am afraid, I put my trust in you.

(Psalms 56:3).

Who Says What?

"Find a place for us to stay".

"You are different! You can not stay here!"

"Can we ask God to send fire to destroy his people?"

"No!, of course not! We should go to another town".

Draw a líne / from the person to what they said, according to the Bible story.

What are YOU thinking?

"I don't know where your doll is and I don't care".

"Get out of my way or I'll hit you".

"I don't want to play with you or your ugly truck".

One of the children in each drawing has been treated poorly.

- How do you think these children are feeling?
- What do you think you would do?
- What do you think Jesus would want you to do?
- Do you think it is hard or easy to be kind to those who act poorly?
- How do you think these children can show kindness?

Turn over the puzzle to find a message from Jesus.

Mix the pieces and then put the puzzle together and remember the Bible story about the widow.

Cut along the solid black lines to make a puzzle.

She gave every- thing she had!

99

"Truly I tell you, this poor widow has put more into the treasury than all the others."

(Mark 12:43)

What do we need?

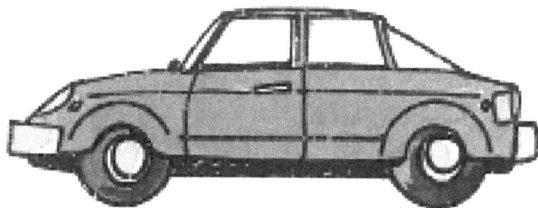

Put a circle around the things that we need to live. Draw an X through the pictures of the things that people enjoy but that it is possible to live without.

How did God care for Elijah?

Cut out the figures on page 127 and paste them in this drawing. Circle what God did to take care of Elijah. Then draw a square around what God sent especially for Elijah.

Jehova shows that He is the only God!

Do you remember the story of Elijah and the false prophets of Baal? Cut off the top of the page along the solid black line, then fold the top of the page forward along the dotted line to see how God responded to the prayer of Elijah.

The _____ of a _____ person is _____ and _____.

(James 5:16b).

Words:
prayer
righteous
powerful
effective

Use the list of words to complete the verse.

Suggestion for the lesson:
The word "righteous" describes a person that tries to live a life free of sin and who obeys God's laws.

Cut out the figures on page 125 and paste them into the boxes.

Elijah ate.

Elijah won the battle against the false prophets and was very tired. Many times people feel moody or sad when they have become very tired.

Elijah sat down to rest under a tree and fell asleep. Maybe you want to take a nap.

An angel brought food and water to Elijah.

Elijah went up to the mountain to listen to God, who told him what to do. God is not far from you. You can pray right now and he hears you. Ask God, your parents, or your Sunday school teacher to advise you so you can always do the right thing.

Elijah listened to God.
105

How do you feel?

Color the face that shows how you feel right now.

Respond "yes" or "no" to the following questions:

YES	NO

Have I done something that I had to use a lot of energy to do?

Do I feel tired?

Am I hungry?

Do I feel that God is far away from me?

1
2
3
4

Did you answer "Yes" to any of the questions? If so, cut out the colored strips on the left side and fold them to cover the questions you answered "Yes" to. Tell someone who can help you about the questions you said "Yes" to and see if they can help you not to have doubts.

When our circumstances change

Draw a circle around all of the things that have changed in your life.

Elijah and Elisha

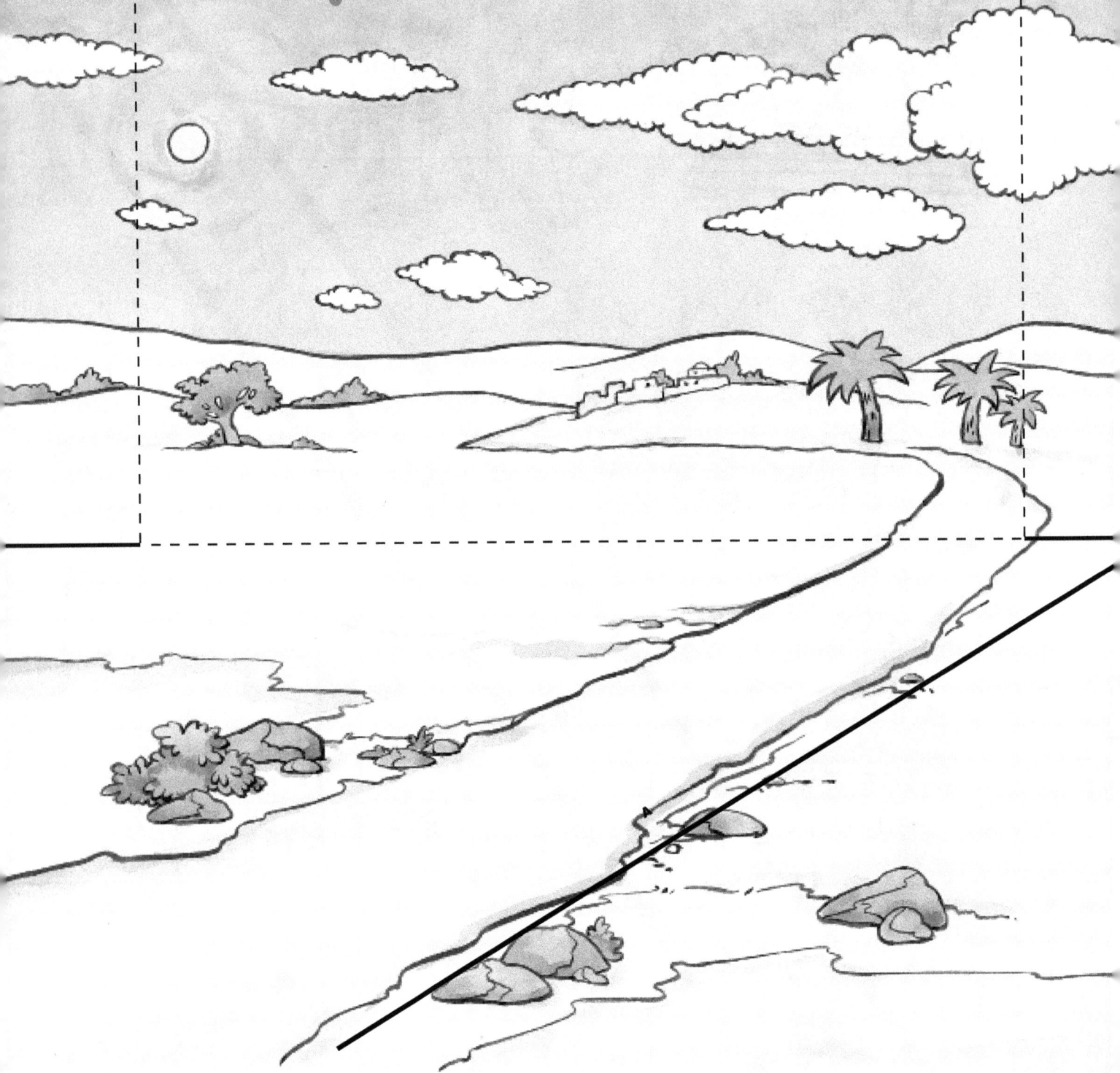

Fold this dotted line backwards. Cut out the solid line marked A and the small lines to the left and right of the page. Fold the paper forward along the dotted line in the middle of the sheet. Then fold the edges back along the vertical dotted lines. Cut out the figures on page 125. Fold along the dotted lines at the bottom of the figures so they will stand. Put the picture of the Chariot of Fire in the cut out line (A). Use the pictures to remember and retell the Bible Story.

Stand Up, Angel!

Color the angel. Then cut out along all the solid black lines. Put glue long the right edge of the dress. Twist it around the back and glue to the opposite edge so that it will stand.

Put glue along this line.

"She will give birth to a son, and you are to give hime the name JESUS, because he will save his people from thier sins." (Matthew 1:21).

Glue   Glue

Glue   Glue

Picture of Jesus' birth

Cut out the stable along the solid black line. Fold along the dotted lines forming folds. Glue the edge of each fold to form pockets. After you cut out the figures below, place the figures in the pockets to create a nativity scene. Now you have a nativity scene to share with your friends and family to show the beautiful story of the birth of Jesus Christ.

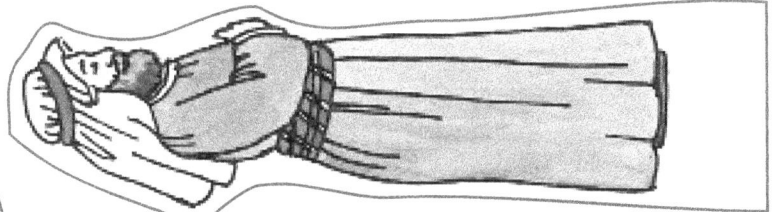

111

2   Tape or Glue   2

1   Tape or Glue   1

3   Tape or Glue   3

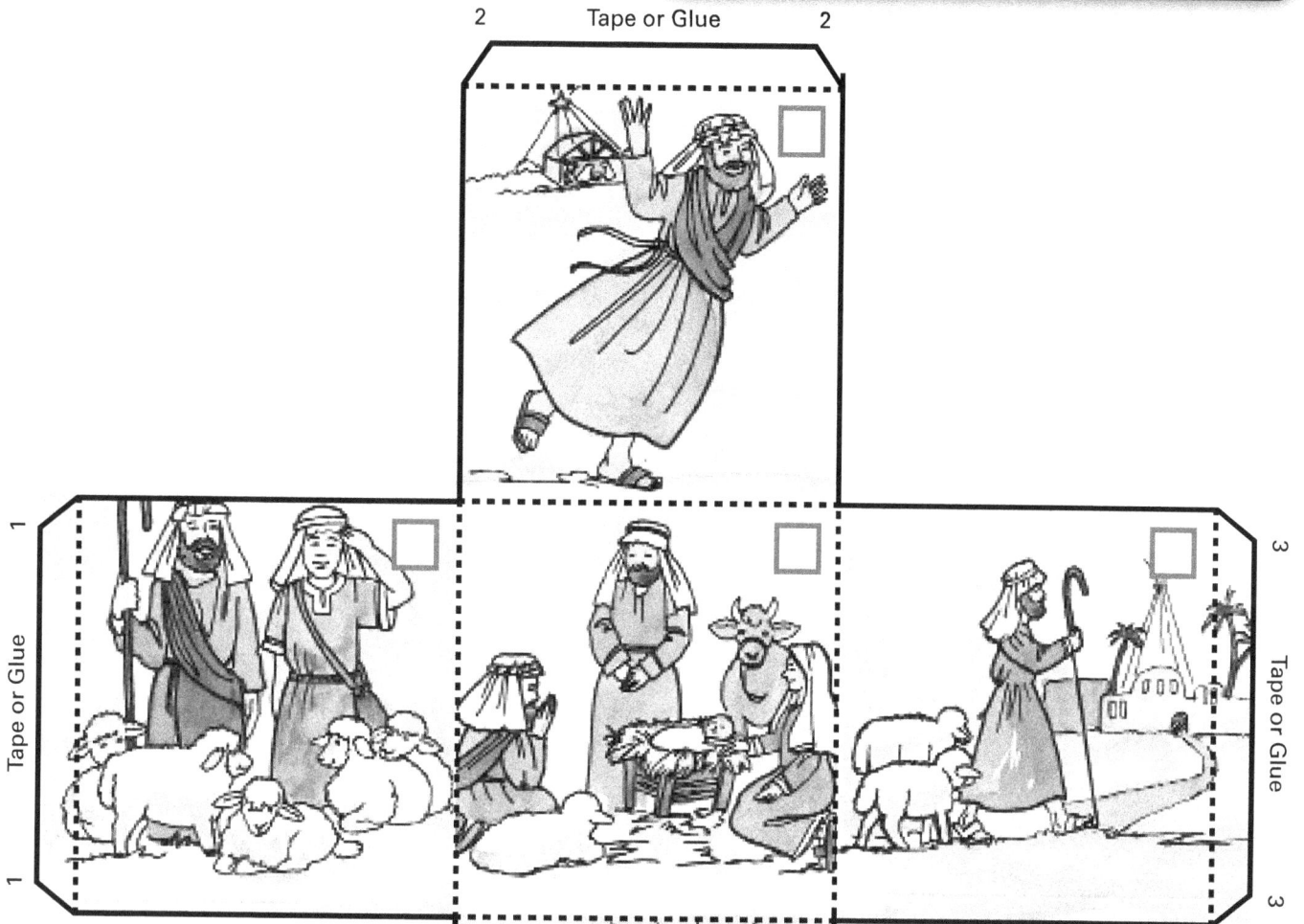

The Shepherds' Cube

Number each box in the order in which the story occurred. Cut out along the solid black lines. Turn the page to reveal the Bible verse so you can understand the true meaning of Christmas. Fold along the dotted lines, and glue the numbered tabs to assemble the cube. Once finished, you can show it to others and tell them the story of the shepherds.

"For God so loved the world that he gave his one and only Son, that whoever believes in him shall not perish but have eternal life."

(John 3:16)

The Gifts of the Magi from the East

"On coming to the house, they saw the child with his mother Mary, and they bowed down and worshiped him. Then they opened their treasures and presented him with gifts of gold, frankincense and myrrh."

(Matthew 2:11)

Cut out the gifts on page 117 and glue them in the hands of the Magi from the East.

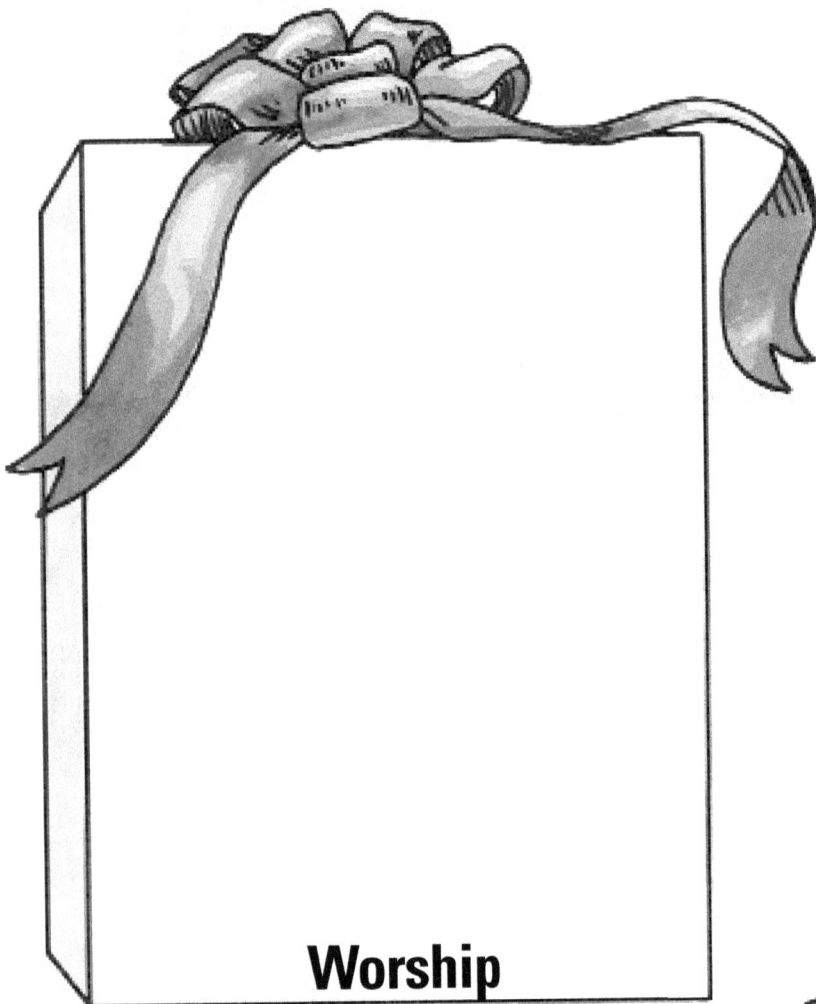

¿What gifts can we give to Jesus?

Worship

"It is more blessed to give than to receive."

(Acts 20:35b).

When you worship and obey God, you give him beautiful gifts. Draw a picture of how you worship God and another of how you obey God.

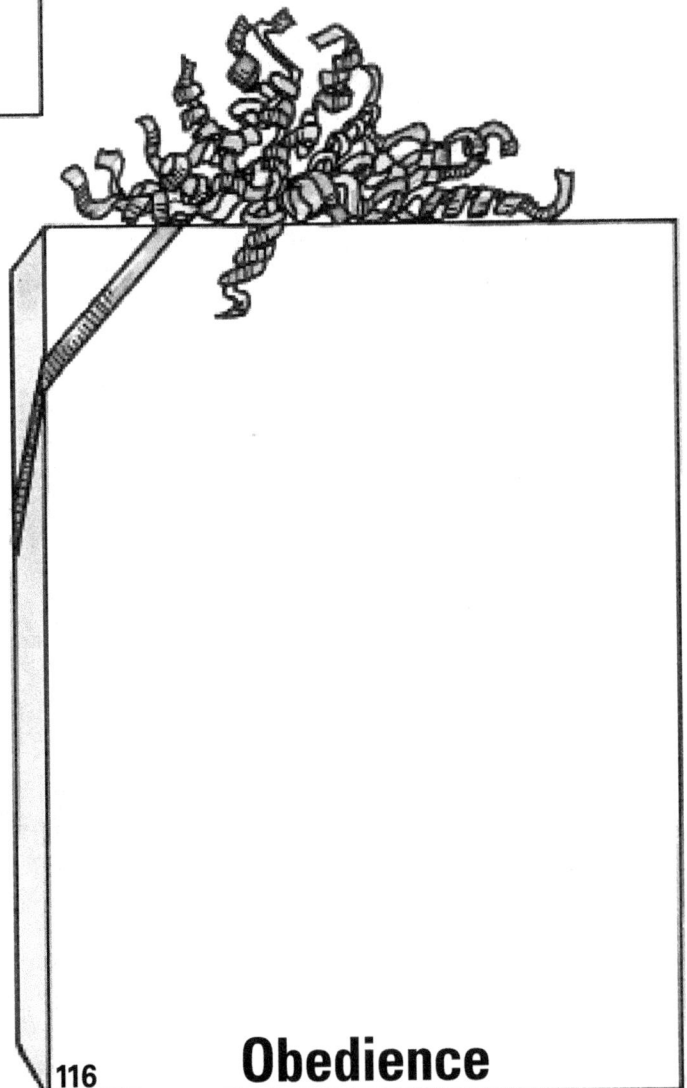

116

Obedience

Memory Verse

Unit I

_____
Name

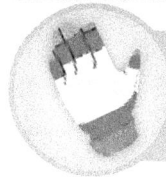

Memory Verse

Unit II

_____
Nambre

Memory Verse

Unit III

_____
Name

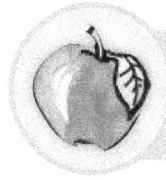

Memory Verse

Unit IV

_____
Name

For use with Lesson 52.
Cut out the gifts and glue them in the
hands of the 3 magi.

Memory Verse

Unit XI

_____
Name

Cut out these
expressions and
glue the faces of
Rachel in the activity
of Lesson 8.

"Obey the LORD your God and follow his commands and decrees that I give you today."
(Deuteronomy 27:10)

"Teach me to do your will, for you are my God;"
(Psalm 143:10)

Unit II

Unit I

"Trust in the LORD with all your heart and lean not on your own understanding; in all your ways submit to him, and he will make your paths straight."
(Proverbs 3:5-6)

"But God demonstrates his own love for us in this: While we were still sinners, Christ died for us."
(Romans 5:8)

Unit IV

Unit III

"For God so loved the world that he gave his one and only Son, that whoever believes in him shall not perish but have eternal life."
(John 3:16)

Unit XI

For use with Lesson 7. Cut out these squares and glue the correct ones into the proper place that show how we can honor our parents.

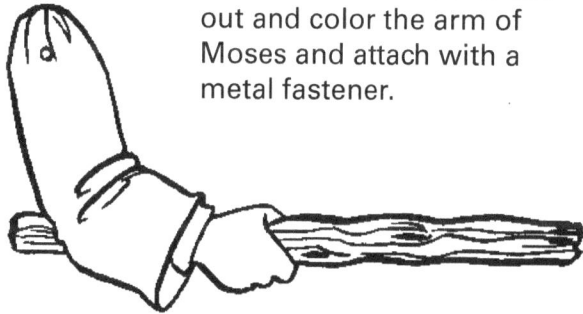

For use with Lesson 4. Cut out and color the arm of Moses and attach with a metal fastener.

Cut out the stars. Use them with the activity in Lesson 9.

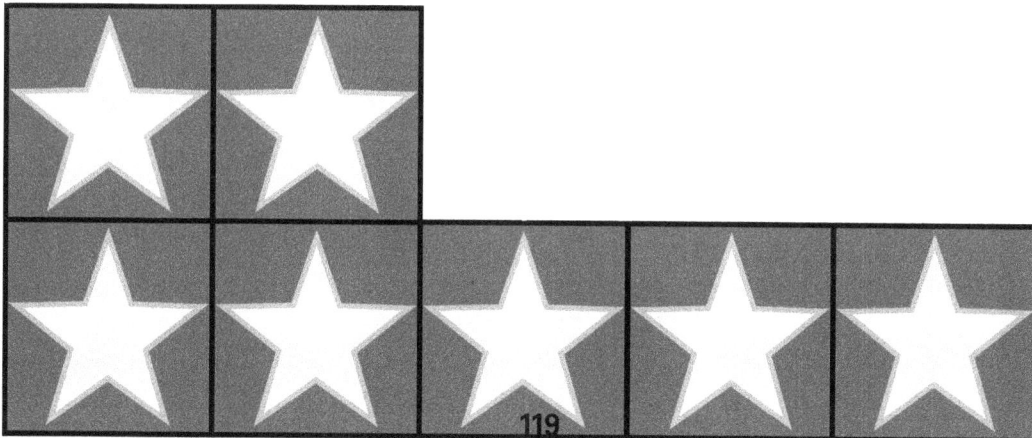

Worship.

Helping to teach Sunday School.

Respect the leaders of the church.

Helping to clean the church.

Bring friends to church.

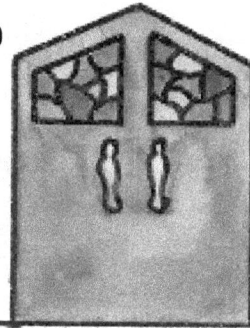

a rich farmer.

the walls of Jerusalem were destroyed.

the people worked together.

the enemies tried to stop him.

let him go and build a new wall.

the King's servant.

his father died.

send your
men to build
the wall.

there are
not enough
workers.

Nehemiah
did most of
the work.

Cut out and use with Lesson 48.

Cut out and use with Lesson 42.

T R U S T

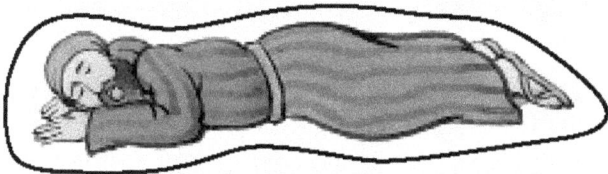

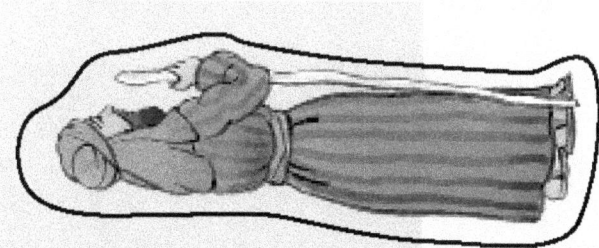

Use with
Lesson 47.

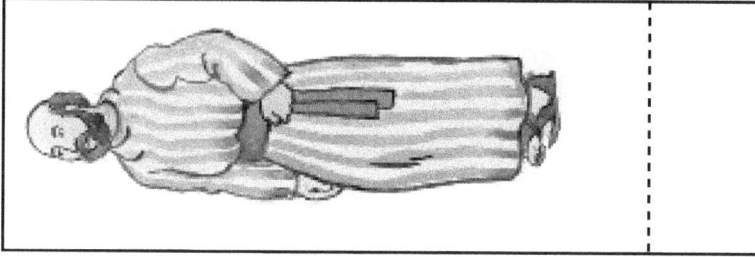

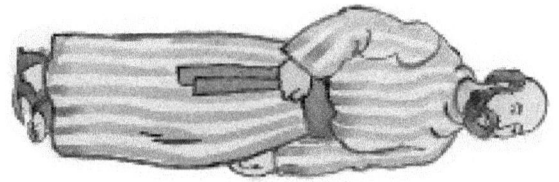

Memory Verse

Unit VIII

_____
Name

Memory Verse

Unit IX

_____
Name

Memory Verse

Unit X

_____
Name

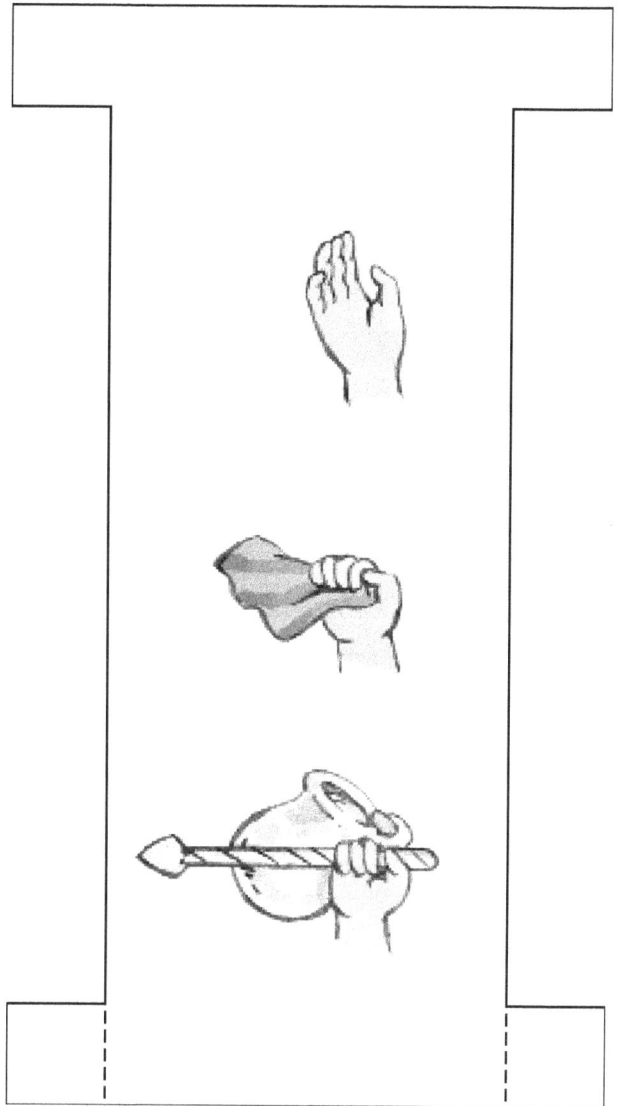

Use with Lesson 39

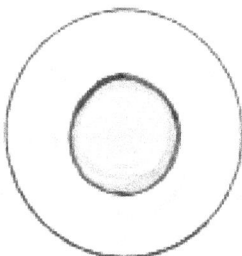

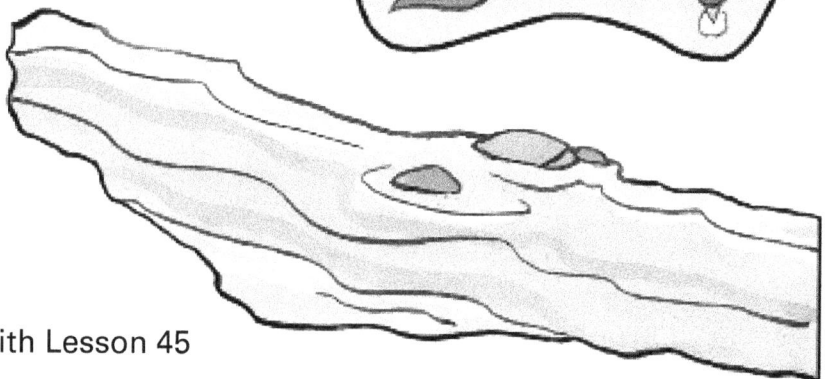

Use with Lesson 45

"... The LORD does not look at the things people look at. People look at the outward appearance, but the LORD looks at the heart."
(1 Samuel 16:7b).

Unit VIII

"... Love the LORD your God with all your heart and with all your soul and with all your mind."

(Matthew 22:37)

Unit IX

"... The prayer of a righteous person is powerful and effective."
(James 5:16b).

Unit X

Memory Verse

Unit V

_____
Name

Memory Verse

Unit VI

_____
Name

Memory Verse

Unit VII

_____
Name

winter

spring

summer

fall

For use with Lesson 23.

The daughter of Jairus

To use with Lesson 29.

"You are my Son".

For use with Lesson 29

"This is my Son, Listen to Him".

Cut out

1

129

2

"In the beginning God created the heavens and the earth."

(Genesis 1:1)

Unit V

"You are my friends if you do what I command".

(John 15:14)

Unit VI

"You, LORD, are forgiving and good, abounding in love to all who call to you".

(Psalm 86:5)

Unit VII

Service Award

For
a
Great
Person

Signature

Service Award

For
a
Great
Person

Signature

Use with Lesson 30.

Use with
Lesson 31.

Search Light,
for use with Lesson 30.

131

Cut along the dotted line.

Cut along the dotted line.

Something
Special for
Someone
Special!

Jesus said: "... whoever wants to become great among you must be your servant" (Mark 10:43).

Cut along the dotted line.

Cut along the dotted line.

Cut along the dotted line.

Something
Special for
Someone
Special!

Jesus said: "... whoever wants to become great among you must be your servant" (Mark 10:43).

Cut along the dotted line.

Gift Cards

www.ingramcontent.com/pod-product-compliance
Lightning Source LLC
Chambersburg PA
CBHW081551040426
42448CB00016B/3283